CASINO
GAMES

John Gollehon

GOLLEHON BOOKS
GRAND RAPIDS, MI

MANUFACTURED IN THE UNITED STATES OF AMERICA

Library of Congress Catalog Card Number: 86-80200

ISBN 0-914839-19-5
(International Standard Book Number)

Cover photos, courtesy of the Desert Inn, Las Vegas

Contents

This book is dedicated to the memory of my beloved mother, Edna Gollehon, who enjoyed our many trips to Nevada with my family.

CHAPTER 1

Baccarat

Baccarat (pronounced bah'-cah-rah), as played in Nevada and Atlantic City, offers the potential player a relatively attractive game in terms of percentages. Plus, there's an excitement that can happen, under the right conditions, that no other game offers. Indeed, once a player overcomes the natural apprehension to play what appears to be a more "sophisticated" game, the unique experience—win or lose, is usually a memorable one. No other game can even come close.

Of all the casino games, baccarat stands out. And for a lot of reasons, not the least of which is the game's snob appeal, and exclusivity.

1

Usually, the baccarat pit is set aside from the main casino area, away from all the "common" games and "common" people . . . in the hopes of luring the casino's best customers—the high rollers and the filthy rich. The baccarat table is the most likely place to find movie and television stars, and all kinds of famous people.

Strangely enough, most casinos are now making a concerted effort to shake the "stuffed shirt" image, and are encouraging the multitude of casino players to try baccarat, and rightfully so. Today, you'll find the high rollers in their best dress, right beside another player in a "Budweiser" tee-shirt. Blue jeans and sneakers are not exactly in vogue at the baccarat tables, but don't be surprised to see a number of shoes under the table cut from "K-Mart" canvas instead of alligator skin. As long as the player's billfold is fat, or there's plenty of credit in the computer, the casino will go along with just about anything.

Regardless, if you ever had visions of rubbing elbows with wealthy corporate executives or famous actors, the baccarat tables might be as close as you'll come. All you have to do is walk up and sit down.

Another factor that gives baccarat a unique excitement is the casino's practice of frequently lifting the limits and letting players go for unheard of risk. Not that it might be of interest to you, but sometimes a player can be found betting $10,000 a hand! It's not uncommon to learn that a particular baccarat table won or lost over $500,000 in a few hours. Like I said, baccarat is different.

Of course, it's not necessary that you wager $10,000

a hand to enjoy the game. Most casinos today have a relatively small $20 minimum bet requirement. For most of us, that $20 minimum requirement might seem a bit steep, but if players on both sides of you are betting thousands at a crack, you might get the feeling you're sitting in the wrong pew.

No matter. You might feel a little tingle when you see a player make such large bets, but you should feel a "jolt" when you see the decision on your own wager, because that's all that really counts. As you can appreciate, $20 isn't chopped liver! If it's *your* bet, it's more important than any other bet on the table!

Another distinction of baccarat is the simplicity of the game. Indeed, baccarat is the casino's easiest game to play. There is virtually no skill or knowledge to be concerned about. Although we'll cover the mechanics of the game later, it's important that you understand here and now that the game is "gosh-awful" easy! If I could get my mother to the table, she could play just as effectively and with the same degree of chance as anyone else.

A Comparison With Other Games

Baccarat makes an interesting comparison with the other casino games in more ways than one.

Most of you are probably aware that there are two hands dealt at the baccarat table, "player" and "banker," and that all players bet on either of the two hands to win, that is . . . to come closer to "9" than the other. Since the player is betting on only one of two possibilities, baccarat compares somewhat to the red or black wager at roulette, and to the "pass" or "don't pass" bet at the craps tables. There are no other bets to make, or at least worth making, so baccarat is essentially a carefree, win or lose, rapid-decision affair.

You pick a side, and then go with it. No different than flipping a coin. And the same deep, mental thought that goes into a coin flip applies to baccarat. Do you try heads, or maybe tails? Shall we bet on "player," or "banker"? Like I said, baccarat is basically a coin-flip, but the *way* the casino plays the game is what sets it apart.

Roulette offers lots of different options for the player, and craps does too. In fact, the number of bets is the only complexing factor of these games, a factor that you don't have to worry about at baccarat.

Blackjack is indeed a game of skill, no question about it. There are several player options that count heavily in the overall expectancy. It's true that blackjack might be the best game in the casino, but it's also the most complicated. Compared to baccarat, it's like piloting a yacht or a row boat. Both games are played with cards, and both boats run on water. One's easy, and one isn't.

Another interesting comparison is the predictability of the game. Just exactly how "random" and how "predictable" is baccarat, compared to the other "games of chance"? Can the player employ any skill at all to change the expectancy of winning or losing? Can a player predict, or at least improve his chances of predicting an outcome? Can a player affect the outcome by his actions? Does indeed the player have any control whatsoever?

The answer is emphatically no. In spite of the fact that the game is played with cards, thereby creating a continually changing expectancy, no one without super-powers could ever detect it. Counting the cards at black-jack and counting the cards at baccarat are like comparing apples and watermelons. Unless you have some "pull" way up beyond the clouds, forget it.

Since baccarat is virtually a purely random game, for all intents and purposes, it makes little difference how you vary your bet size, or for that matter, whether you choose the "player" position or "banker." Baccarat is a game of luck, with a constant negative expectancy riding on every decision.

Over the long term—lots and lots of decisions, the game is going to beat you. But since the casino settles for such a small percentage as their advantage in the game, there will be some incredible successes (and failures) in store for you in *short-term* play. Unfortunately, these short-term sessions run into long-term vulnerability. As you learn to play, remember to limit your exposure. Take any winnings and run!

Above all, remember that you're bucking odds against you, no matter how small, so be careful.

Casino studies have shown that the average wager at the baccarat tables is considerably less than in prior years. This means that more and more players who are *not* high rollers are playing and enjoying the game. Unless you can't afford the casino's $20 minimum bet, don't let it intimidate you. And don't be intimidated by the casino's formal approach to the game. So what if the dealers are all dressed in tuxedos. Who cares if the baccarat room is lavish and rich in decor. Remem-

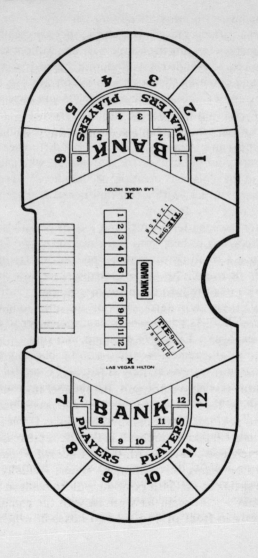

ber, the casino is doing it for *you*.

I've been playing baccarat for years. It took me a long time to interest my wife in playing, and more appropriately, to overcome her apprehensive fear. Finally, I had to literally drag her into the baccarat room and seat her at the table myself. Once she learned the casino's simple rules and method of play, she relaxed and enjoyed herself. Now, I can't keep her away! She loves it. And so do I.

How To Play

As mentioned earlier, baccarat is by far the easiest game in the casino. With the exception of "third card" rules that we'll cover in a few pages, there is virtually nothing to study, nothing to practice, no tough decisions to make. Indeed, skill is not a factor.

As you walk up to a baccarat table, you'll first notice that the table is larger than you would expect for only 12 players and 3 dealers. Although most tables today do seat 12 players, some casinos have chosen a still larger table to accommodate 14 players. If you're sitting at the last player position, the number in front of you will be 15, not 14. You're the 14th player but in the 15th position. Make sense? The reason is because all casinos eliminate number 13. For the same reasons that hotels don't have a 13th floor. I guess I wouldn't want to be sitting in position 13 either. Actually, if you're sitting at the 14th position, you're really at the 13th, and . . . . well, let's get on with the game.

Directly in front of you are two boxes in which to

make your bets. The box closest to you is for betting that the player will win, and the box farthest from you is for betting that the banker will win the next hand.

In case you're a rank amateur in the casino, I don't want to mislead you with the term "boxes." The casino doesn't have a real, three-dimensional box on the table. I'm talking about *two*-dimensional "boxes" that are printed on the table's felt covering. The boxes represent an "area" for you to make your bet. A "section," if you will, that distinguishes your wagers from those of the other players.

Two dealers, standing over the casino's supply of chips, are responsible for paying your bet when it wins, and removing it when it loses. Each dealer works a particular end of the table. One of the dealers is in charge of the players in position 1 through 6, and the other dealer is responsible for all the players at the other end, positions 7 through 12. The third dealer of the team is the "caller," and is responsible for directing the game, the deal, the outcome, and the passing of the shoe.

The shoe is no different from what is used at the blackjack tables, and represents an efficient way to "deal" cards from an 8-deck supply. The cards are standard playing cards without jokers. The only difference from what you might buy at the local drug store is the backing. Generally, the casino has their logo on the backs in some graphic fashion. But the sides of the cards that count are nothing special.

The shoe facilitates the dealing of cards by a slight downward pressure with your fingers. The top card will exit easily by the shoe's tilted and bottom-curved design. Can you appreciate that dealing cards by hand from eight decks, especially by inexperienced players, could at times be a little messy? The shoe is simply a convenience device, that also helps to insure an honest game.

So, baccarat is a card-game, as you might have already gathered, where initially 4 cards are dealt, two each to a player-hand and banker-hand. The object of the game is to come closest to 9. The magic number at the blackjack tables is "21," but at baccarat we're looking for "9." It's possible that one of the two hands, or none, or both, will receive another card at the instruction of the dealer, but since the third card is the only complicated part of the game, we'll cover it in more detail later in this chapter.

Card Values

Baccarat has its own rules about card values. And now's the time to learn them. All number cards 2 through 9, count as their face value. The ace counts only as 1, and all 10-value cards including face-cards count as 0. So, if the player-hand includes a 3 and 4-value card, the total is 7. If the banker-hand is an 8-value card and a face-card, the total is 8. Remember, the face-card has no value. In this particular situation, the banker-hand would win over the player, 8 over 7.

Whenever the card values total 10 to 19, such as an 8 and 6-value card, "10" is subtracted from the total so that in this case, the hand-value is 4 (14 - 10 = 4). If the hand totals 20 to 29, such as a 7, 9, and 6-value card, "20" is subtracted from the total so that in this case, the hand value is 2 (7 + 9 + 6 = 22 − 20 =

2). In the case of three 10-value cards, the hand total is 0. Remember, the hand total cannot exceed 9. *An easy way to quickly determine the value of a hand greater than 9 is to simply take the last digit of the number, such as 9 for 19, 0 for 20, and 7 for 17.*

Here are some examples for you to look at:

$4 + 4 = 8$ $10 + K = 0$

$K + 8 = 8$ $5 + 9 = 4$

$K + Q = 0$ $3 + 5 = 8$

$A + J = 1$ $7 + 4 = 1$

$6 + 6 = 2$ $K + K + 10 = 0$

$3 + 2 + 9 = 4$ $K + K + 7 = 7$

Dealing The Hand

What makes baccarat interesting is the player's participation. As you can see so far, the game is elementary. But to make it more exciting, the casino wants you to join in by dealing the cards from the shoe, although you don't have to if you don't want to. If you don't want to deal (perhaps during the first few moments while you're still learning) simply tell the dealer you wish to pass the shoe. No big deal. Later on, you'll probably want to participate, and actually look forward to getting the shoe.

Here's the way it works.

The shoe passes around the table in a counter-clockwise direction. The player holding the shoe is considered the "banker," although you're not taking any additional risk, and technically you're not the banker anyhow, but merely represent the banker-hand.

Many players confuse baccarat with its dangerous European "cousin," Chemin de Fer, where the player with the shoe does indeed take a risk by actually "banking" the bets of the other players. But in Nevada-style baccarat, the casino is always the real banker. The designation of the player with the shoe as banker, is a mere formality.

So, in this paragraph, we'll refer to the player holding the shoe as the banker. The first action is the instruction of the dealer, "Card for the player." On this command, the banker slides a card out of the shoe, face-down, and pushes it to the dealer. Incidentally, *all* cards are dealt face-down. Next, the dealer tells the banker, "Card for the banker." Instead of pushing the card to the dealer again, the banker tucks the card under the corner of the shoe. This series of actions is repeated . . . Card for the player, and another card for the banker, again tucked under the shoe's corner. Now, the dealer has two cards in front of him, face-down, and representing the player's hand. The banker has two cards tucked under the shoe, representing the banker's hand.

Next, the dealer will determine which player at the table has made the largest bet on "player," and will give that particular player the two cards representing the player's hand. The player will turn over the cards, noting the total, and then toss the cards back to the dealer.

A silly formality, you surmise, but it's the way of the game. The player with the biggest bet on "player" has been given the "honor" or privilege to be the first to see the cards.

The dealer repositions the player's hand directly in front of him and announces the total. Next, the banker removes his cards that were tucked under the shoe, looks at the cards, and then tosses them to the dealer also. The banker's cards are positioned above the player's cards in front of the dealer and the total is announced to all the players. At this point, the game might not be over, depending on whether or not a third card is required.

It's likely that either the player-hand, or the banker-hand, or both hands will require a third card before a decision is made. We'll go into more detail about third-card rules later on, but for now, let's complete the action.

Incidentally, **what's nice about the third-card rules is that the player who's acting as banker *does not need to know the third-card rules*. The dealer once again will instruct the banker when to deal another card, if indeed it's required by the game's strict rules.**

Had you worried, right? You probably thought you would have to memorize some complicated schedule in order to play this game. No, there's nothing to memorize. But most players, as they become more experienced, desire to learn the third-card rules because it makes the game so much more interesting. But remember, there's no guess-work on your part, or any rules at all to know. The dealer will always tell you exactly what to do.

Let's say that the dealer does in fact tell you, "Another card for the player." Then slip another card out of the shoe and push this third card to the dealer. The player-hand always acts first if a third card is called for. Next, you might be told, "Another card for the banker." That's your cue to deliver another card to the dealer, and now you're finished. Neither hand can be more than three cards. The dealer will promptly announce the winner, such as, "Banker wins, 5 over 3."

Since we're assuming that you were the banker (holding the shoe), you would have won the bet had you placed your wager on the banker-hand. It's customary at baccarat for the banker to bet on the banker-hand, although it's not a rule. Most players do, however, again for the reason that it appears to be just another formality.

Any other player at the table who also bet on banker would also have won their bet. And as long as the banker continues to win, the player with the shoe continues to be the banker. When the banker-hand ultimately loses, the player passes the shoe to the next player on his right, and that player becomes the new banker.

So far, the game has been made much more elaborate than need be, but as you'll learn by actually playing, this added routine is the game's trademark of formality. It's a formal game, in a formal setting, with formal rules.

I should mention here that I've occasionally referred to the caller as "dealer," not to be confused with the dealers opposite the caller who only handle the chips. The caller is a dealer also, in fact, the three-member team of dealers usually alternate and share the calling duties throughout their work-shift.

The 5% Commission

Mathematically, the banker-hand has a slight edge over the player-hand because of the way that the third-card rules have been established. It would make sense therefore, to always bet on the banker-hand. But the casino has come up with a neat solution to this discrepancy by charging a commission to the player each time he bets on banker *and wins*. The commission helps to equalize the difference in probabilities, and gives both bets nearly the same odds of winning.

Although the commission rate is 5%, the actual "damages" to the player is not nearly 5% over long-term play, because the commission is only charged on the banker-hand *when it wins*, and remember, the banker-hand has a built-in advantage over the player-hand anyhow.

We'll discuss the house percentage at baccarat in great detail later on, but if you can't wait, I won't make you finger through all the pages. The banker-hand gives the casino a 1.06% edge, while the player-hand is worth 1.24% to the casino. So, as you can see, in spite of the commission "equalizer," the banker is the best hand, but both bets favor the house.

Keeping track of the commission is the job of the two dealers standing across from the caller, and directly over the casino's stash of chips. In front of the chips is a row of commission boxes, representing each player's position at the table.

Each time a player makes a bet on banker (and wins), a 5% commission is noted in his respective box with "token" chips. When the shoe is exhausted, it's customary for each player to settle up the accrued commissions that are due. Always be sure that you have enough money in front of you to cover your debt. It would be embarrassing if you didn't have enough money to pay it, and ended up having to wash dishes. Frankly, I'm not sure what the casino would do if you forgot about the commissions, but to be safe, always make sure you have it covered.

As the commissions are being paid, the caller will assemble all the cards, literally mix them on the table (another formal distinction of the game), stack the eight decks, and then turn over the top card. That card-value indicates the number of cards to be "burned" (removed from the top of the stack) and discarded into the bowl at the center of the table where all played cards are accumulated.

Now we're ready to go through the shoe again, starting with the same banker if the banker-hand won the last hand, or by passing the shoe to the next player if the last winning hand was "player."

Rules Of The Game

First of all, the easiest rule to remember is that an 8 or 9 is called a "natural" and represents the highest hands. If either the bank-hand or the player-hand has an 8 or 9, neither hand draws a third card. Any natural stops the hand and a decision is called as to the winner.

It's possible that a natural 8 could lose to a natural 9, but a natural 9 cannot lose. Of course, the natural

9 could tie with another natural 9, and the result is called a "tie." With all the formality to this game, you would think they could come up with a more "deluxe" term, but when both hands end up with the same number, any number, it's just called a plain tie. When the hands tie, there is no action on your bet. After a tie, you are free to increase or decrease your bet, remove it, or change it.

Player-Hand Rules

Now, let's look at a typical chart of the rules as provided by the casino. Most casino managers agree that the baccarat rule-card is somewhat confusing in its design, terminology, and lack of information. Surprisingly, virtually all casinos use this same card. Later on, we'll look at a rule-card as I've designed, that's much easier to understand.

According to the casino's chart, the player always stands on a hand-total of 6 or 7. OK, that's easy enough. Now we can remember that the player always stands on 6-7-8-9.

The rule-card also states that the player must draw a third card whenever the hand totals 1-2-3-4-5-10. Wait a minute! What's a 10! Why the hell do the casino's rule-cards say "10" when we all know that there isn't such a number at baccarat. What the casino wishes to imply is that the player-hand always draws a third card for hand totals of 0-1-2-3-4-5. Makes more sense and it's easier to remember.

Regarding the third card, the player-hand always acts

PLAYER

HAVING	
1-2-3-4-5-10	DRAWS A CARD
6-7	STANDS
8-9	NATURAL, Banker cannot draw.

BANKER

HAVING	**DRAWS** WHEN GIVING	**DOES NOT DRAW** WHEN GIVING
1-2-10	**DRAWS**	
3	1-2-3-4-5-6-7-9-10	8
4	2-3-4-5-6-7	1-8-9-10
5	4-5-6-7	1-2-3-8-9-10
6	6-7	1-2-3-4-5-8-9-10
7	STANDS	
8-9	NATURAL, Player cannot draw.	

PICTURES AND TENS HAVE NO VALUE

If Player takes no card, Banker stands on 6

first. When the player-hand is concluded, then it's the banker's turn. So technically, we're half-way home. We now have learned that the player-hand always draws a third card when the total is 0-1-2-3-4-5. Always stands on 6-7-8-9. But remember that 8 or 9 stops the hand; the banker cannot draw, and the hand is over.

Banker-Hand Rules

The rules for the banker-hand are far more complicated, but let's see if we can simplify them.

The banker always draws a third card with a hand-total of 0-1-2. And always stands on 7-8-9. But if the banker's hand is 3-4-5-6, the mandate of drawing a third card depends on the *player's* third card. According to the chart, if a banker-hand totals 3, and if the player's third card was 1-2-3-4-5-6-7-9-10, then the banker-hand must draw a third card. What the casino's rule-card fails to mention is that if the player did not draw a third card, then the banker draws anyhow. Only a player-hand's third-card of 8 will stop the hand when the banker has 3.

Incidentally, the casino's term, "WHEN GIVING," means "when giving the player-hand a third card." The values shown under "DRAWS," and "DOES NOT DRAW," represent the player-hand's third-card value.

It's much easier to understand the banker-hand rules if you study only the right side of the chart. Ignore the middle column. The right-side column with the heading "DOES NOT DRAW," indicates the only action that will *stop the hand*. Baccarat dealers are taught the game in much this same manner. For example, if the banker-hand is 5, the hand will stop only if the player-hand received a third card and the value of that card was 0-1-2-3-8-9. Otherwise, the banker always draws a third card. The banker will draw even if the player did not draw a third card.

An Easier Rule-Card To Use

To help you remember the rules, here's my version of the rule-card that makes much more sense.

PLAYER

STANDS ON 6-7-8-9.
OTHERWISE, DRAWS THIRD CARD.
8-9 STOPS THE HAND.

BANKER

STANDS ON 7-8-9 AND WHEN:

HAVING	AND PLAYER'S THIRD CARD IS
3	8
4	0-1-8-9
5	0-1-2-3-8-9
6	0-1-2-3-4-5-8-9 (or no card)

OTHERWISE DRAWS THIRD CARD.
8-9 STOPS THE HAND.

Remember, the player's third-card value under "AND PLAYER'S THIRD CARD IS" **always stops the hand.**

Practice Hands

Here are some baccarat hands, indicating the correct action. Review each example until you fully understand the rules. At least give it a try.

Player has 0. Banker has 4. Player draws 8. Banker must stand. Player wins 8 over 4. (Note that the player's third-card draw of 8 stopped the hand.)

Player has 2. Banker has 1. Player draws 5. Banker draws 6. Tie hand, 7 to 7. Nobody wins.

Player has 7. Banker has 5. Player must stand. Banker draws 6. Player wins 7 over 1.

Player has 9. Banker has 6. Player wins 9 over 6. (Note that the player's natural 9 stopped the hand.)

Player has 7. Banker has 6. Player must stand. Banker must stand. Player wins 7 over 6. (Note that banker must stand because player did not draw third card.)

Player has 5. Banker has 8. Banker wins 8 over 5.

Player has 3. Banker has 6. Player draws 6. Banker draws 2. Player wins 9 over 8. (Note that banker had to draw because only a third card for the player of 6-7 will *not* stop the hand when the banker has 6.)

Player has 1. Banker has 3. Player draws 8. Banker must stand. Player wins 9 over 3.

Player has 7. Banker has 5. Player must stand. Banker draws 3. Banker wins 8 over 7.

Player has 5. Banker has 3. Player draws 9. Banker draws 0. Player wins 4 over 3. (Note that the banker's third card was a face-card.)

Player has 2. Banker has 7. Player draws a 3. Banker must stand. Banker wins 7 over 5.

Player has 6. Banker has 4. Player must stand. Banker draws 3. Banker wins 7 over 6.

Player has 4. Banker has 4. Player draws 5. Banker draws 9. Player wins 9 over 3.

Player has 1. Banker has 5. Player draws 0. Banker must stand. Banker wins 5 over 1.

The Mathematics Of Baccarat

The probability of winning the banker-hand is 44.62%, and of winning the player-hand is 45.86%. The remainder percentage of 9.52% represents the times that the hands tie.

As you can see, the banker does indeed enjoy an advantage over the player of 1.24%. If it would not be for the commission charged to winning banker-hands, it could be said that the casino has a 1.24% house advantage when the player bets on the player-hand, and the player himself has a 1.24% advantage when he bets on the banker-hand. Under these conditions (without commission), it would behoove the player to always bet on the banker-hand and eventually own the casino.

The Actual "Cost" Of Commission

To understand how the 5% commission charged to winning banker-hands actually affects the banker-hand's percentage, let's use a simple coin-flip as an example. Instead of "banker" and "player" where the probabilities are not the same, we'll be using the terms "heads" and "tails" where the probabilities are indeed the same.

If the casino is sponsoring our hypothetical coin-flip, you can be assured they would not offer 1 to 1 odds on your wagers. Otherwise, over long-term play, the casino would not show any profit. So, let's say that the casino's rules state that they will pay you 1 to 1 odds and charge you a 5% commission only when you win. Contrary to what most people think, the casino's advantage is such a contest is only 2½%, not 5%. *They'll be earning 5% on only one-half of all wagers.*

To compute house advantage, you must always consider the player's net loss over all the probabilities for the game. In this case, it's 2 . . . head or tails. In the case of roulette, all the probabilities total 38, because there are 38 compartments where the ball might fall. So, for our coin-flip example, the house makes 2½% over the course of two probabilities (two flips).

The best way to confirm this easy example is to make a bet on both heads and tails. That way, you are sure to "win." You have wagered $1 on heads and $1 on tails. The casino will give you 95 cents for your winning wager, plus you retain the original $1 bet, but you lose the other bet for $1. Your net loss is 5 cents based on $2 in total bets. That's a 2½% advantage for the house (.05/2).

Now, to make our coin-flip more like baccarat, let's say that the casino's rules state that they will pay you 1 to 1 odds but charge you a commission of 5% *on only one-half of your winning bets.* That's more like baccarat because the casino charges you the 5% commission only when the banker-hand wins, not the player-hand. In this case, the casino has cut their advantage to 1¼%. And in a sense, that's what the 5% commission at baccarat really costs the player. Technically, because the probabilities of the banker-hand and player-hand differ, our example is a little off, but the message should be clear.

In any game where the probability is the same on every hand, the casino's advantage applies to every hand. So, back to the case of our coin-flip, the 1¼% advantage applies to wagers on either heads or tails. But in the case of baccarat, since no commission is charged to the player-hand when it wins, we would have to double our 1¼% advantage back to 2½% if we only apply it to the banker-hand, in order for the overall house advantage to be maintained.

Since the true house advantage on the banker-hand is 1.06%, the difference in percentage that the player has lost because of the commission is 2.3% (1.24% + 1.06%). The discrepancy (2.5% vs. 2.3%) is because of the differing probabilities that we called attention to earlier.

The player-hand is worth 1.24% to the house. The banker-hand as we noted is only 1.06%. Therefore, we can conclude that the banker-hand is still a better bet for the player, although it should be noted that both hands favor the casino. Since we can assume that the player makes a nearly equal number of bets on both banker and player over a long course of play, the overall house advantage for the game can be judged as 1.15% (1.06% + 1.24% ÷ 2).

As you can now see, the 5% commission charged against winning banker-hands is really not a 5% house advantage as many players believe. We went about proving it the long way so that you wouldn't have any doubt. Actually, the short way to prove the "cost" of the 5% commission is to simply take .95 (win less commission) times the 45.86 probability of the banker-hand winning, and subtract the 44.62 probability of the player-hand winning, then subtract the 1.24 banker-hand advantage before commission. But that's too easy.

$$.95 \times 45.86 - 44.62 - 1.24 = 2.3$$

Regardless of the numbers, the important thing for you to realize from all this is that baccarat is indeed an attractive game in terms of minimal house advantage. Only the pass-line bet at craps with single or double odds proves to be a better wager.

Accordingly, it's unfortunate that so many players avoid baccarat because of the intimidating formality. And yes, the minimum bet of $20 can also be a strong deterrent. But it's important to realize that the game is about as good as your going to get, anywhere in the casino.

But don't misunderstand me. I certainly don't mean to suggest that you're going to *win more*. More appropriately, I'm suggesting that you should *lose less*. But not knowing the manner of your play, I really can't even confirm the latter.

For the player who practices common sense, discipline, and wise money management, baccarat shouldn't take a very big bite out of your wallet. And who knows, maybe in short-term play, you might get lucky and hit it big!

But remember, no matter how small the percentage against you, the longer you play, the more likely you will lose.

The Casino's "Drop" Percentage

The casinos have a better way of proving the house advantage than resorting to hard-core mathematics.

All casinos monitor table action every day and report the findings to casino administrators on a weekly computer print-out that shows the handle, hold, and percentage of each game. The "handle" represents the total amount of all bets, the "hold" is the casino's winnings based on the game's advantage, and can be expressed simply as a "percentage."

The casino knows exactly what their percentages are for slot machines because each machine registers every coin inserted and every coin awarded. But at the table games, an exact number of bets is difficult to determine. Generally, the casino is concerned about the "drop" percentage which is based on the total amount of money in cash and credit slips that each table takes in through the metal slot on each table game. As a rule, the casinos figure to win about 20% of the drop each and every day. Don't confuse this figure with the house percentage. The drop percentage is more correctly a measure of the amount of a player's original stake that he ultimately parts with. The house percentage is the advantage the game provides the casino that works on every wager, every hand, every roll, and every spin.

Generally, the casino can figure the hold percentage based on the drop and chip-count at each table. Although it's certainly not as accurate as slot machines, the casino can come close based on the plain fact that they've been in the gambling business for over 50 years. Experience!

What I'm leading up to is somewhat discouraging news. I've been privy to the casino's computer print-outs from time to time and am somewhat surprised at the figures for baccarat. Although the baccarat numbers vary by a greater degree than the other table games, the figures support a higher percentage than what has been mathematically determined.

Based on these casino records, it would appear that baccarat is more on the order of 3%, but mathematically we know better. Perhaps the reason for the higher casino figures is the action on tie bets that we haven't really discussed yet. And for good reason. The casino will pay 9 *for* 1 odds (which is really 8 *to* 1) if you bet that a hand will tie and it does. The casino advantage on this stupid bet is over 14%! Don't even consider it. But it's possible that many players do indeed make an occasional tie bet and this could be the reason for the casino's apparent higher percentages overall.

Shills And High Rollers

Baccarat in Nevada and Atlantic City generates substantial income for the casinos, but not because the house percentage is big, and not because of the number of bets. We know that the house advantage is minimal, on the order of 1.15%. Certainly, that small of a percentage can't be the reason for the casino's big take.

If you walk by the baccarat pit, especially in the morning or afternoon hours, you'll notice little activity. Usually, only one table out of three is running, and even then, there are few real players. The casino employs "shills," as they're known, to help start a game. The shills use the casino's money, and have no serious interest in the game. Sometimes, the shills are attractive women, chosen to lure the high rollers, most of whom, apparently are men.

The casino, and the shills themselves, make no effort to hide their identity. It's not a scam against the player, it's merely a tactic. No one wants to play baccarat alone.

Frankly, I too prefer to play the game with real players, not shills, who have a sincere, financial interest in the game. Accordingly, the best time to play is in the late evening hours, when the tables are nearly full and the action really heats up.

Getting back to our original theme, it is indeed the high rollers who generate the substantial income for the house. Not the percentage. Not the *number* of players. And here's the point. A typical baccarat table can generate nearly 40 hands per hour. Lots of decisions. I'm not suggesting the game is *too* fast . . . just fast!

If the casino is lucky and many of the seats are filled with high rollers, it's possible that over $5,000 in total wagers will be risked on every hand. Sometimes, a single player will bet that amount, and teamed up with the other players, it's possible that over $20,000 could be decided on the flip of a card! And here's where the casino really makes their money. Don't let the "small" 1.15% advantage fool you.

Let's be conservative, and say that on a busy night, the average total-table handle is $5,000 per hand. That's $57.50 for the casino based on the 1.15% advantage. Based on an equally conservative 30 hands per hour, the casino will net $1,725 per hour! Sure, sometimes the casino will turn up on the short end. But over long-term play, thousands and thousands of hands, the casino knows that they have the winning edge.

With the casino's high cost of running baccarat (it's the most expensive to operate per table), it's doubtful that the game could endure, at least at the currently low percentage, *if not for the high rollers*.

If most of the players were making $20 to $200 bets as I do, the game's profitability would suffer, and either the rules would be changed to give the casino a bigger edge, or the game would shut down.

For you and me, let's think of the high rollers as subsidizing our play. We can take part in a game with a remarkably low percentage against us; in fact, a game that can really be enjoyed, without having to make ridiculously large wagers. All of us who indeed make *sensible* bets should join together and thank the high rollers for the game's preservation.

Mini-Baccarat

"Real" baccarat is what we've just discussed, played at the big tables in a "pit" usually away from the main casino area.

But some casinos offer "mini-baccarat" that other than the rules, has little resemblance to big-table baccarat, and offers nowhere near the excitement and formality. We'll discuss the game for you, but I can't recommend that you play it.

The mini-baccarat table is about the same size and configuration as a blackjack table and is situated in the main casino area. A single dealer performs all the actions; the player does not participate. Watching the dealer handle the cards—usually very fast, can become downright boring in a matter of moments.

The suspense of big-table baccarat is missing; the player doesn't handle the shoe; and the pace is simply too fast!

Sometimes, the casino will alter the rules a might, and take ties. Although the betting minimum is usually one or two dollars, the commission rate might be too high to afford a true 5% computation. If the minimum commisison is 25 cents, then the minimum bet for a 5% commission would have to be $5. If you're betting $1, and pay a 25-cent commission, that's 25%! Not smart! If you do elect to play mini-baccarat, be sure to inquire as to the minimum commission requirement, and the minimum bet size. Be sure that ties are a "push," as they *should* be.

CHAPTER 2

Blackjack

Blackjack is played with a standard deck of 52 playing cards, in fact the same "Bee" brand that you can buy in any drug store, made by the U.S. Playing Card Co. Jokers are removed.

You and any other players at your table (up to 7) are playing against the casino, represented by a dealer who merely deals the cards, and has no other "interest" in the game. The dealer's actions are mandatory, based on strict game rules. Technically, the game could be dealt by a machine or a monkey, since no playing skill is required.

The only possible "skill" to worry about is cheating,

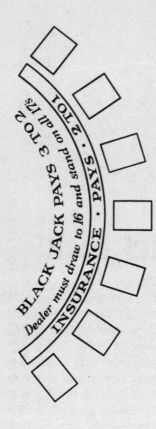

This is a typical layout of a blackjack table on the Las Vegas "Strip." Notice that the dealer must stand on *all* 17's. "All" 17's means that any total of 17, including an ace counted as 11 such as ace-6, stops the draw. This rule favors the player.

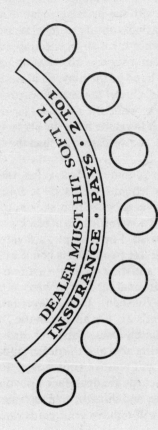

This layout is typical of most casinos in "Downtown" Las Vegas and in Northern Nevada. Notice that the dealer must hit soft 17 (any total of 17 including an ace counted as 11). This rule is a disadvantage to the player, and should be avoided where possible.

but frankly, it happens very rarely, if ever, especially at the larger, well-known casinos. Many years ago, perhaps. But today, with the priceless value of a gaming license, and the casino's ability to generate substantial income honestly, cheating is an inconceivable enemy.

Cards are dealt from a shoe (a box containing more than one deck) or by hand to the player and the dealer, each getting two cards. One of the dealer's cards is face-up for everyone to see, while the other is face-down.

The simple object of the game is for the player to have a hand that totals "21" or is closer to 21 than the dealer's hand.

The "number" cards count as face-value, the "picture" cards count as 10, and the "ace" is counted as either 1 or 11, whichever is better to make or approach 21. *The four suits have no significance in blackjack;* only the number value is used. For example, a 6-value card and a Queen count as 16; two Queens count as 20.

If the player is not satisfied with his first two cards, he may ask for an additional card, or as many as he likes until he "stands" (is finished). If the player takes too many cards and exceeds 21, it's an automatic "bust," and the player immediately loses. Toss your cards on the table between the betting area and the dealer, indicating the bust. The dealer will remove your wager. In some cases, all the player's cards are dealt face-up; you never need to touch the cards, and shouldn't. In this case, when you bust, the dealer will remove your cards (and your wager) for you.

When all players at the table have acted on their hand, the dealer turns over the card dealt face-down (hole-card) and stands only if the total is 17 or more. The dealer is required to draw cards until the hand totals at least 17 or more. If the dealer "busts" in the process, all players who did not "bust" themselves are automatic and immediate winners.

If however, the dealer does not bust and has a hand that totals between 17 and 21 (which it must, because the dealer draws to make at least 17, and more than 21 is a bust) the hand is compared to the player's to see which is closer to 21. Whichever is closer, wins. If both the player and the dealer have the same total, it's called a "push" (a tie) and there's no decision on the bet. In that case, the player is free to remove the wager, increase it, or decrease it. Only after a push, or after a win, can the player again touch the chips in his betting area. Never touch your bet after a game has begun. Casino personnel are very suspicious.

Now, read this brief section again carefully until you fully understand it. It's the essence of the game! If you're wondering on what hand-totals to draw cards, or at what point to stop drawing, don't worry about it now. We'll cover that later, at precisely the right time, for all possible hand combinations.

All bets that win are paid at 1 to 1 odds, "even money." If you bet $5, you win $5, and so on. However, if the player's first two cards are a 10-value card and an ace, it's called a "Blackjack" (wins outright) and is paid at 3 to 2 odds. You'll receive $15 to your $10 bet. *The 10-value card does not need to be a picture-card.* A "ten" of spades or any other suit is worth just as much as a Jack, Queen, or King. Any 10-value card and an ace make a Blackjack.

If the dealer receives a Blackjack on the first two cards,

the player loses at even money (only the amount of their wager) unless the player also has a Blackjack, in which case it's a push.

The only other exception to the even money wagers is called "Insurance." Here's how it works. If the dealer's upcard is an ace, the dealer will ask all the players if they wish to take insurance. To do that, you bet an additional amount up to one-half of your original wager, betting that the dealer does in fact have a 10-card underneath, in which case you win 2 to 1 for your side-bet. The dealer always "peeks" at the hole card if an ace is showing to determine if he has a Blackjack, before the players are given the option of taking more cards.

In most casinos, the dealer also checks the hole-card if a 10-value card is showing, again to determine if the dealer has a Blackjack.

Today however, many casinos no longer allow "peeking" at the hole card (unless an ace is showing) to discourage collusion between the dealer and a player, attempting to cheat the casino. It's possible a dealer could "signal" the hole-card value to a player and thereby give the player a tremendous advantage.

The bottom line on insurance is *don't do it!* It's a silly bet that only increases the house percentage.

Hit Or Stand Motions

To recap, the most important option the player has is to either "hit" or "stand." Your way of indicating to the dealer that you wish to hit or stand depends on whether the cards are dealt face-up or face-down. Some casinos deal all the player's cards face-up, other casinos deal the player's first two cards face-down.

At tables where the cards are dealt face-up, the player never needs to touch the cards. To signal a hit, the player may do either of two motions.

I prefer to point at the cards, actually touching the table with my finger about two to three inches from the cards. This way, there's no question that I want another card. Unfortunately, some casinos frown on this action for whatever illogical reason.

The other motion is to simply bring your hand toward you in a scooping motion. But be sure you do this over the table, so the "eye in the sky" can see it to record. (The casino's video-tape cameras are there to protect both the casino and the player. Don't be intimidated by them. Every table is in fine focus.)

If you don't want another card, I recommend that you simply put out your hand, towards the dealer, as if to indicate "stop." The casino recommends a horizontal motion as if you're wiping a piece of glass above the table.

However, it's been my experience that the latter motion can easily be confused with the opposite signal, especially if the player is particularly sloppy with his motions. Try my way.

At tables where the cards are dealt face-down, you obviously must pick up the cards to read your hand. If you do not want another card, simply place both cards face-down on the table and slightly under your bet. In most casinos it's all right to simply place the cards within close proximity of your wager.

If you want a hit, keep the cards in your hand until it's

your turn to play. Then, lightly "scrape" the card edges on the table, towards you.

Incidentally, it makes no difference whether the cards are dealt face-down or face-up in blackjack. This ain't poker! But, it does make a significant difference to card-counting that we'll discuss later.

Splitting

Another important option for the player is to "split" identical cards in your original hand, such as a pair of 8's. When this option is available, the player does not just automatically do it! The decision to split or not to split your pair depends on whether or not it will be an advantage to you.

When we get to our "basic strategy" later in this book we'll detail each possible pair combination in comparison to the dealer's up-card, and make the decisions for you.

For now, however, let's prematurely make two important rules abundantly clear: **Never, never, never split 10-value cards, such as two face-cards, and never split 5's. Always split aces and 8's!** If you're an inexperienced player, see if you can quickly understand the solid reasoning behind these two important rules.*

When you wish to split your cards at a face-down table, simply position your cards face-up and behind your bet (to the dealer's side). Then, make another wager of the same size and place it directly *beside* (not on top

---

*Splitting 10-value cards is my favorite example of greed. You're throwing away an excellent hand! Players who split a 20 should have their head examined.

of) your original bet. At a face-up table, you only need to make a new bet inside the betting circle to indicate the split, since your cards are already in position.

The dealer will know that you are splitting the pair, and will give you two more cards, one to each card you split, in effect establishing two new hands that are working for you. If you receive another identical card, you may split again, and you'll have three hands in play.

However, all casinos do not allow the re-splitting of aces. To make matters worse, after the dealer has given one card to each of the split aces, the hands stand. The casino will not afford you the option of hitting. Regardless, splitting aces is still a strong player advantage. Always do it.

Double Down

Here's an option that figures significantly in the player's ability to adjust the percentages. You may "double down" on your first two cards by making an additional bet up to the amount of your original wager and receive *only one card* from the dealer. One hit.

Obviously, the time to double your bet is when you have a hand-total of 10 or 11 and the dealer's up-card is 6 or less. That's the ideal situation. Another 10-value card will give you a 20 or 21. Even an 8 or 9 will give you a pat hand (17 or better). That's the reason we told you earlier never to split 5's. The two 5-value cards give you a hand-total of 10, and that's usually a good time to double down.

We'll give you the complete basic strategy for doubling

down, and all the other player options, later in this book. You'll know exactly when to do it, and when not to.

As I've mentioned before, the casino industry has been negligent in their efforts to standardize game rules. Perhaps it's an element of competition that shouldn't be standardized. Whatever, the rules do vary, and doubling down is a good example.

Some casinos limit double down to only 10 or 11. Still other casinos will allow double down on *any two cards,* and that's a big advantage to the player, as you'll learn later.

Unfortunately, most casinos not only have different rules, they *change* their rules about as often as your gas bill goes up. So the best solution is to simply ask before you play.

Surrender

"Surrender" is an option that few players understand or readily use. Probably because most casinos, until recently, did not offer it or promote it. Now, as blackjack players become more sophisticated and discriminating, casinos are turning to it more and more.

This is what it means to the player. If you don't like your first two cards, and that happens a lot, you can "surrender" the hand and lose only one-half of your bet. To enforce surrender, simply state "surrender" to the dealer, and throw in your cards. The dealer will remove half of your bet and you're out of the woods. It's that simple.

I refuse to play blackjack in any casino without surrender rules. I don't want to hit a 15 or 16 against the dealer's 10. The only time surrender is not allowed is when a dealer has a blackjack. So wait for the dealer to peek when an ace or 10-value card is up. If the dealer does not have a blackjack, you're allowed to surrender.

A Soft Hand

Any hand that includes an ace has two values . . . a soft value and a hard value. If our hand is an ace-6, the soft value is 17, the hard value is 7.

Although it doesn't come up that often, there's a decision to make whether or not to hit a soft 17, 18, or 19. Usually, a soft 20 is good enough and the player stands. But it's important to remember that *a soft-17 will not bust.* A 10-value card will simply make the soft-17 hard. Depending on the dealer's up-card, we actually may want to double down on a soft 17, if the casino allows it. We'll give you the basic strategy for soft hands in the following pages.

Earlier in this chapter, I told you that the dealer is required to draw to 16 and stand on 17. That's the basic rule on the "strip" in Las Vegas but in Northern Nevada and "downtown" Vegas the rule is altered somewhat, requiring the dealer to hit a soft 17. It's a nasty ploy, and definitely a disadvantage to the player.

On the table layout in "strip" casinos, it clearly states, "the dealer must stand on *all* 17's." Much better!

Basic Strategy

Before we look at the charts, let's apply some good old-fashioned "horse-sense" and see if we can understand the reasoning behind them. You'll be able to remember the strategies so much easier if you understand why they work!

First, let's identify the potential "bust" hands as "stiffs." And it's a great term for them. When the dealer gives you a 12, 13, 14, 15, or 16, you got "stiffed!" If your hand is 15 or 16, you've got one of the two worst hands possible, and especially tough if the dealer's upcard is a 7 or higher.

Don't screw it up anymore than it already is by *not* hitting it, or *not* surrendering it if you can.

If your cards total 17, 18, 19, or 20, it's a "pat" hand. It's decent. Although 17 and 18 may be good enough to stand on, they certainly won't get all the "marbles" all the time. 19's, 20's, and Blackjack's are the real "goodies" you're looking for.

Judging by what we now understand to be the object of the game, and the basic game rules themselves, it would appear that the biggest casino advantage is the fact that the player has to draw *before* the dealer does.

That simple fact accounts for a hefty 7% advantage to the house.* So many inexperienced players sensing

---

*Since all casinos pay 3 to 2 for a Blackjack, this effectively lowers the 7% house advantage to a little less than 5%.

Player options based on "basic strategy," including hitting, standing, doubling, and splitting for both hard and soft hands will lower the house percentage to about ½%. This number cannot be determined precisely because of variations in rules from one casino to another, and the frequent rule changes that occur. In addition, a multiple-deck game will add at least ½% to the casino's edge, regardless of the player's counting technique.

Mediocre strategy may give the casino another 2-3% advantage. A poor strategy may increase the casino's edge to 5% or more!

that problem, elect to never hit a stiff for fear of busting. That dumb little ploy is worth about 3% to the house. We can work down the 7% advantage other ways, but not *that* way!

Now, see if you can identify the "good" cards and the "bad" cards for the player. It's important. Think about it.

It would seem obvious that all 10-cards are good, because they help give you 20's, and pair-up nicely with an ace for a Blackjack. Sure, **10-cards are good!**

What about 2's, 3's, 4's, 5's, and 6's? They help to promote those lousy stiffs, right? And more importantly, they can improve a dealer's stiff hand without necessarily busting. **2's, 3's, 4's, 5's, and 6's are indeed, bad cards!**

Although we're getting a little ahead of ourselves, the object of *counting* is to determine how many 10-value cards and how many 2's, 3's, 4's, 5's, and 6's are *left in the deck,* based on how many you've seen *come out of the deck*.

When the ratio of 10-cards to "little cards" is high, the player has an advantage. If there are too many little cards left in the deck, the dealer has a distinct advantage.

As you read the charts coming up, you'll notice that our strategy depends on *both* our hand total and the dealer's up-card.

Multiple-deck games will affect our percentages and the strategies that follow, but only to a limited degree. However, it can be concluded that multiple-deck games are indeed an advantage to the dealer, not to the player!

Hit Or Stand Strategy For Stiffs

PLAYER'S HARD HAND	DEALER'S UP-CARD									
	2	3	4	5	6	7	8	9	10	A
16										
15										
14	S	T	A	N	D		H	I	T	
13										
12	H	IT								

ALWAYS STAND ON 17 OR BETTER!

Our strategy for hitting or standing with stiffs is really quite simple as you can see.

Always hit a stiff when the dealer has a 7 or higher. Remember it as 7-UP, and you'll never forget it.

Always stand on a stiff when the dealer has a 6 or less showing, with the exception of 12. The dealer does not have a pat hand (with the exception of ace-6) so there is a good possibility the dealer will bust.

Always stand on 17 or better. Never, even in your wildest dreams hit 17! Dealers must alert pit bosses in many casinos when a player hits 17 or better. See if you can guess why.

Always draw a card on 11 or less. You might actually double down or split depending on the card values, but at the very least, you'll always hit it.

Incidentally, the hit and stand rules apply not only to your original hand, *but to your hand at any time.* For example, if your original hand is 10-4 against the dealer's 10, you hit it. You receive a 2. Now you have 16. According to the chart, you must continue hitting (until you have 17 or better).

Sure, the odds are against you, but you had a losing hand in the first place. Over the long term, you'll reduce the casino's initial advantage we talked about by about 2½% with correct hitting and standing strategy. Reducing the percentages against you is the name of the game.

Hard Double Down Strategy

PLAYER'S HARD HAND	DEALER'S UP-CARD									
	2	3	4	5	6	7	8	9	10	A
11			D	O	U	B	L	E		
10				D	O	W	N			
9							H	I	T	

Notice that the player should **always double down on 11,** regardless of the dealer's up-card.

Doubling on 10 is restricted to a dealer's up-card of 9 or lower. If the dealer's up-card is 10 or an ace, it's obviously too risky.

Some experts differ on the rule for 9, ironically. Our position must be to **only double down on 9 if the dealer's** up-card is 3, 4, 5, or 6.

It's a mute point in many casinos (especially Northern Nevada) where doubling is limited to 10 or 11. Doubling after you have split is equally restricted in many casinos. Ask before you play to be sure you understand the rules in a particular casino. **Always seek out the best playing conditions.**

Proper strategy for hard double downs (and for soft doubling that we'll cover under ''Soft Hand Strategy'') further reduces the casino percentage by about 1½%. We're getting there!

Splitting Strategy

PLAYER'S HAND	DEALER'S UP-CARD									
	2	3	4	5	6	7	8	9	10	A
A-A			S	P	L	I	T			
10-10			S	T	A	N	D			
9-9										
8-8			S	P	L	I	T			
7-7										
6-6							H	I	T	
5-5	D	O	U	B	L	E				
4-4							H	I	T	
3-3			S	PL	I	T				
2-2										

Most computer-aided strategies for splitting pairs are randomly defined, with no symmetry to recognize. It's exceedingly difficult for the layman player to remember. In fact, most player-errors in basic strategy are made when splitting.

Accordingly, I've taken the liberty of simplifying our splitting strategy to make it much easier to remember, with only a minuscule trade-off in accuracy.

Since the overall advantage to the player for correct splitting is less than ½% (the smallest of all the player options) there's no reason to be alarmed. The simplification of an otherwise complex strategy is justifiably appropriate for this text.

Here's how to remember our special splitting strategy:

Always split aces and 8's. Never split 10's, 5's and 4's.

Treat 5-5 as 10 and follow our double down rule — double if the dealer shows 9 or less, otherwise just hit.

Split 9's when the dealer has 9 or less, split 7's when the dealer has 7 or less, and split 6's when the dealer has 6 or less. Remember that the dealer's up-card is always the same or less than the card you're splitting with 6's, 7's, and 9's.

Only split 3's and 2's when the dealer's up-card is 4, 5, 6, or 7. Otherwise just hit.

Soft Hand Strategy

PLAYER'S SOFT HAND	DEALER'S UP-CARD									
	2	3	4	5	6	7	8	9	10	A
A-9 (20)			S	T	A	N	D			
A-8 (19)										
A-7 (18)				D						
A-6 (17)				O						
A-5 (16)	H			U						
A-4 (15)	I			B			H	I	T	
A-3 (14)	T			L						
A-2 (13)				E						

Once again, our "soft" strategy has been ever-so-slightly simplified to make it easier for you to remember.

Always stand on a soft 19 and 20. They represent good hands regardless of the dealer's up-card.

Always double down (if it's allowed) on a soft 13 through 18 when the dealer has a 4, 5, or 6 showing. Otherwise hit 13 through 17.

A soft 18 is the most difficult to remember because there are three options. **Always double down on a soft 18 when the dealer is showing a 4, 5, or 6 (just like the smaller soft hands) and hit it when the dealer is showing a 9, 10, or ace.**

With a 9 or higher up-card, the dealer may have a better hand, so it does pay to try to improve your soft 18. Remember, you can't bust any soft hand with a single hit. However, if you end up with a poor draw, such as a 5, you must hit it again (hard 13) and take your chances.

Surrender Strategy

The rules for surrender are so simple, we don't need a chart to show you.

PLAYER'S HAND	DEALER'S UP-CARD
15-16 (hard)	7-8-9-10-A

Many gaming experts disagree on surrendering a 15 or 16 to the dealer's 7 or 8 up-card. Most all agree to surrender on a 9, 10, or ace up.

This is *my* book, so I'm telling you *my way* to do it. **Surrender a 15 or 16 stiff (except 8-8) when the dealer has a 7 or higher up-card,** *if you're playing in a casino where they allow it.* You should be.

And wouldn't you know it, the casinos can't agree on surrender rules either. Some allow you to surrender your hand only after the dealer has checked a 10 or ace up-card for Blackjack. A few other casinos, very few, will allow the surrender before the hole-card is checked. It's worth nearly 1% to you. So look for it. Don't hesitate to lose half of your bet with a bad hand. It beats losing it all!

The Advantage Of Basic Strategy

Now that we have presented a solid, basic strategy, it's important that you memorize the charts, so you'll know exactly what to do with every conceivable hand and dealer up-card.

The instant you see your cards, make your decision right away! Don't guess. Follow basic strategy exactly! There's no reason to ponder.

Find a deck around the house and practice! *Don't bet a dollar until you've mastered the strategy.*

Like anything else, our basic strategy charts will at first appear too complicated to memorize. But as you dig into it, and practice, your "skill" should become second nature. Yes, your effectiveness can only be measured by how much you practice. I'm sure it took Terry Bradshaw a long time to learn how to throw a football. And how long do you suppose Earl Anthony practiced throwing strikes? I know, this isn't football or bowling, but it *is* a game! How well you are prepared will have a direct and lasting effect on your confidence level. And you know how important that is! Make a decision right now whether or not you'll be able to do it. **You must have confidence in yourself before you can have any confidence in your game.**

What advantage does the casino have against a player with good, basic strategy? I was hoping you wouldn't ask me that question! Every gaming expert in the world has tried to come up with a nifty number. But no one can pinpoint it.

Even with today's advanced, high-speed, powerful

computers, no one can give you a precise casino advantage because of the rule extremes that vary significantly from one casino to another.

Is the game one-deck or a multiple-shoe?

Does the dealer stand on all 17's or hit a soft 17?

Can I double down on any two cards, or is it limited to 10 or 11?

Can I double after I split?

Can I resplit aces?

Is surrender available?

Can I surrender before the dealer checks his hole-card?

And as I've mentioned before, even if you know the game rules in a particular casino, they may change tomorrow. Totally unstable!

Suppose we could find an exact percentage based on a certain set of rules, and we could if we wanted to. Now what?

Do you play a basic strategy absolutely perfect? I doubt it. Are you mediocre? Probably. If you're a poor player, you'll give back most of the casino's 5% advantage or more.

Do you see the point? No player is infallible. To what degree do we correctly apply basic strategy? It's a significant question in determining the casino's edge.

Still another matter that you must consider when weighing the casino's percentage is the fact that it's built on long-term decisions. Nothing says the percentages can't vary 10% or more during the short term! There are incredible fluctuations that can occur, especially with a single-deck game.

Hopefully, all the big fluctuations will fall in your favor, but don't be so naive as to think you can't lose ten hands in a row. You can, and you will . . . some-time. There are no guarantees over the *short term.* You must understand this!

An arbitrary percentage of 1% (an acceptable number) only tells us that over a *very long period*, we will probably lose $1 for every $100 we bet. It would theoretically take 10,000 plays for the casino to take all our money, betting $1 a hand. So you can see the 1%, although a very small number, will wipe you out, eventually. Don't be misled by little numbers!

I like to consider the casino advantage as ½% based on average playing conditions for an average player using basic strategy. My number is about as useless as any other expert's number, because of all the reasons we've just cited.

Of course, if an "exceptional" player has found a casino with "exceptional" game rules, blackjack can be considered "even." With surrender, the player may actually have a slight edge.

I got a big kick out of a leading expert's number for the casino percentage. He made a big deal out of it as if the "media" should report on his findings!

Not to embarrass him, I'll change it a little but keep the same number of digits. That's the ridiculous part. He says blackjack with basic strategy is .347%!

There's no qualification as to the particular game rules, and why carry it out to three places? It's a totally useless, meaningless number, unless you plan on playing literally tens of thousands of hands under optimum playing conditions without a single error in strategy.

What we *can* determine from our analysis however, is that blackjack is about as safe to play as craps. I'm not saying it's safe, I'm saying it's about the same. Using basic strategy (with 95% accuracy) and under "decent" playing conditions, I rate both games a toss-up.

However, if a player goes one step further and masters a count strategy to identify the fluctuations while they're occuring, blackjack is indeed a better game. Knowing to increase your bet size when the opportunity is there, and laying back when the opportunity is gone, is the tremendous advantage to keeping track of the cards.

Keeping track of the *dice* is a waste of time. Previous rolls have no effect on future rolls. But at the blackjack table, previous cards *do indeed* have an effect on future cards.

Counting The Cards

Most gaming experts who have authored other books, steadfastly believe that you must keep a running track of all cards that have been dealt, follow an ever-changing basic strategy, and then adjust your betting for that rare moment (about 5% of the time) when the odds have shifted in your favor. In a nutshell, that's the computer-proven, mathematical approach to beating the game.

In order to keep an accurate "count" of the dealt cards, you must be able to concentrate fully. The casino won't let you drag in a portable computer terminal. Even a pencil and pad of paper are a no-no. To use the popular "count" systems widely advertised today, you simply must have a good memory recall, and the stamina to stay with it.

If you can't keep the count as you're suppose to, and

you flat-out refuse to learn "basic strategy," then black-jack will end up about a 5% game for the house, or better!

I'm not trying to scare you away. I'm just giving it to you like it is. You see, **blackjack is a unique game that requires two special skills. You already know about one of them—basic strategy. The other is counting. The professional player who might actually have a long-term advantage over the casino is a master at both.**

Unfortunately, a high-level counting strategy, fully detailed, is far beyond the scope of this text. None-the-less, I'm going to give you the raw basics of a powerful counting system later on, for when you might be ready for it. At least you won't have to go out and buy another book!

For now, in order to realize at least something from the counting concept, I'll show you a way to take a "little" advantage from it. A way that's remarkably easy. But it's a compromise. And yes, there will be some work to do. Practicing your "second" skill will be important, and hopefully a "fun" experience for you.

Many players today presume that keeping track of the cards is a relatively new concept. Surprisingly, the first count strategy was developed many years ago in 1963, by Dr. Edward O. Thorp, and widely publicized in his famous book, *Beat the Dealer.* Thorp based his revolutionary concept on work performed nearly ten years earlier by Roger Baldwin and a team of researchers.

Baldwin developed a basic strategy for player options, much as we know it today. Thorp devised a system for counting 10-value cards, working in conjunction with Julian H. Braun, a computer expert at IBM. Braun became active in blackjack analysis on his own, and made significant individual contributions.

The original work of these principal founders has seen little refinement over the years. A testimony to the accuracy of their work. Baldwin, Thorp, and Braun deserve the lion's share of the credit for pioneering count systems and basic strategy.

Today, there are literally hundreds of blackjack systems available, some at ridiculously high prices, but all based on the original work of this elite group.

The Point-Count

We've already hinted to you what counting is and why it works. In essence, we know that little cards help the dealer, and larger cards help the player. Based on that critical aspect, it would logically follow that you must keep track of the little cards and the big cards as they appear, and ascertain the remaining cards in the deck by simple subtraction.

Thorp's original 10-count system was never seriously challenged for accuracy. Indeed, who would be dumb enough to challenge a computer! The problem however, arose immediately. It was too complicated for the layman player to use! Thorp recommended a computation of 10-cards and little cards in the form of a ratio. The computation had to be done in the player's head. No easy matter.

Finally, a balanced system of counting was devised whereby a "minus" number is assigned to a large card, and a "plus" number assigned to a small card. Forgetting the ratios, the player would simply count the plus numbers and the minus numbers to determine the deck construction at any moment.

Today, the systems that are plus and minus numbers are commonly called "point-count" systems and are generally regarded as the most powerful.

PLUS (COUNT +1)					MINUS (COUNT −1)				
2	3	4	5	6	7	8	9	10	A
1	1	1	1	1	0	0	0	1	1

To actually use this counting strategy, the player literally counts the cards as they appear from the shoe (or hand), counting " + 1" for the little cards and " − 1" for the big ones. Only the 10-value cards and the ace are worth counting as plus values in this case; the middle values, 7, 8, and 9, are incidental and not worth tracking.

You can now see why card counters demand a "cards-up" game. It's much easier to count them! When the cards are dealt face-down, the counter must wait until a player busts to see those particular cards, or until the other players settle their wagers. It's also the reason why sharp counters always want to play at "third base." That's the last position at the table—to the player's far left, and allows the counter to see more cards exposed before he must act on his hand.

The advantage to counting is two-fold. For one, *the counter will adjust the size of his bet as the count changes.* When the count is a high plus-value, he will increase his bet-size because many small cards have been removed from the deck, out of ratio to the normal distribution. Similarly, when the count he is mentally keeping turns to a low negative-value, he will greatly reduce his bet, or perhaps wait out the shuffle—maybe leave the table entirely. He has a "negative expectancy" so why play?

The other advantage to counting is *the player's ability to change basic strategy as the count changes.* For example, if the counter knows an unusually large number of 10-value cards are out of the deck, he may decide not to double down, even though he has an 11-value hand and would certainly double on it under normal circumstances.

In fact, a professional counter follows an ever-changing basic strategy as his count continually fluctuates. He has memorized and recalls data from at least five or six different strategies for all the player options; computes the new count as each card appears; adjusts his bets in relation to this count; watches out for the pit bosses; and tunes-out all other distractions of the casino.

Holy Toledo!

You're right if you think this takes the fun out of the game for the great majority of players. You can expect a mild headache. But it's the counter's way of work. For them, it's serious business.

When I'm playing, I use a count strategy called the "Imperial Count" that I devised a few years ago and detailed in *Pay the Line*. Although that particular count scheme differs vastly from the point-count I've just revealed, and is considerably easier to master, it too is beyond the scope of a beginner's book.

Counting With "Over-View"

Without counting, the best a player can do is master basic strategy for the player options, and shop the casinos for the best game rules. With surrender, it's possible to conclude that the player can find a *nearly* "even" game (which isn't bad) but the temptation to take it one step further without complications, is the next logical progression in skill.

Here's how you can use counting, without actually counting!

In my own studies, I've determined that a good counting skill is the most useful when the ratio of little cards to big cards is dramatically off kelter. Obviously, that's the time to really act. You might bet a little heavier, or you might leave the table, depending on whether the deviation is good or bad for the player.

Start out by just tracking the little cards—2, 3, 4, 5, and 6. *On average, two of every five cards should be a little one.* If you see ten cards on the table, four of them should be small. If it turns out that six or seven of them are small, you have an edge *at that moment*. If only one or two cards are small, the dealer retains the advantage.

Surprisingly, when such fluctuations occur in a large degree, it will appear almost obvious to the player who is *only aware of what to look for, without actually keeping the count.* This practice is what I call a counting "over-view." Most all dealers are trained to look for it, and so are the pit bosses, especially at "downtown" casinos or wherever single decks are in play.

The best example of a counting over-view happened

to me February 1985 at the Desert Inn, Las Vegas. The "DI" deals a six-deck shoe, not much of a treat for card counters as I'll explain later. In any event, I played a dealer head-on (no other players at the table) and noticed the first few hands were all 5's, 6's, a few 4's, 7's and 8's . . . not a single face-card! After ten or so hands, all but a few of the 24 5-value cards had been dealt! The odds of that happening are staggering! Since a 5-value card is the worst for the player of all the little cards, it gave me a tremendous advantage for the rest of the shoe. The 5's were nearly all gone! How could anyone not have noticed!

Eventually, the shoe began to "right" itself somewhat, and I ended up winning only a token amount. I'm telling you this because there's a big lesson in it. Even under superbly ideal conditions, there was no guarantee, for me or for anyone. Sure, I won, but it turned out to be less than the expectancy. Anything can happen in short-term play!

The important thing here is my awareness of the swing in expectancy from negative to positive. Now, you can be aware of it too . . . and use it to your advantage!

Press up your winning bets, up to but not more than three times, when the little cards seem to be out in abundance; lay back, or walk away when the 10's and ace's seem exhausted.

A chart of detailed betting levels would not be appropriate here, since for simplicity sake, there is no detail to the counting strategy. However, most casinos with one or two decks, and a haven for counters, will generally shuffle the deck *at any time* when a player suddenly increases his bet size by more than three times.

My recommendation is that you increase your winning bets to the degree that you see a relative number of small cards in bunches, or favorably out of ratio to the remaining deck. A modest player advantage might signal a bet that's 50% more than your previous winning wager. That's all. And even though I'm counting, I make it a point *not to press* a losing wager.

For most players, you'll be able to read a table's complexion after a few hours of playing time. Better yet, after a few hours of practicing at home! You'll get a pretty good idea of the remaining deck construction simply by a review of the dealt cards, noting any unusual excess or deficiency in small cards.

Large fluctuations occur rarely. Most of the time, the deck runs fairly normal in the way the little cards and big cards are arranged. **The likelihood of a large fluctuation, good or bad, is greater in single and two-deck games, as opposed to the 6-deck and 8-deck shoes.** That's why most counters prefer a single deck. Can you appreciate that the large quantity of cards in the multiple-deck shoe tends to thin out the fluctuations? And even if we've found a big swing in the ratio, the remaining cards in the multiple-deck will throw off our expectancy. More so, a multiple-deck is difficult to count. For the beginner, it's not going to be that significant whether you're playing a single deck or shoe table. But as you progress in experience, look for the few single-deck games that remain, and watch for the fluctuations that can occur.

A Comparison Of Playing Conditions
In Atlantic City And Nevada

If you look for a single-deck game in Atlantic City, you might as well look for the Himalayas. As of this writing, mostly 6-deck and 8-deck games prevail. One casino is dealing a few 4-deck games; that's the best you can do!

Although the New Jersey Casino Control Commission requires that game rules are uniformly the same among casinos, the number of decks is not considered a "rule." However, the commission does require that all cards are dealt from a shoe, not by hand. Supposedly, any casino could install a one-deck shoe. The common excuse is that it would cut down on the number of decisions per hour.

Atlantic City casinos have a wide base of customers. So many, in fact, that they really don't need a single-deck game to lure players. They already have them.

In 1981, the Casino Control Commission obliged the casinos in their petition to prohibit "surrender" entirely. The casinos claimed they were losing too much money! Chuckle, chuckle.

Incidentally, the regulatory agency also prohibits sports-betting, poker, and keno.

Don't look for much improvement in playing conditions out East until there's less regulation and more casinos. In Nevada, there's no stymie to competition since the casinos are pretty much free to set the game rules as they please. Plus, there's a lot of casinos, drawing from a smaller market of players.

Good, healthy competition in any marketplace, free of regulation, invariably benefits the customer. Accordingly, you'll find that most of the real professional gamblers play in Nevada. They know where the best rules are.

How To Bet

The subject of betting—all kinds of progressions and theories, has been known to fill entire books!

Some authors recommend that you press up your bets when you're losing, to recoup the losses, based on the dangerous idea that you can't possibly lose ten hands in a row. You can. And you will, sometime. Never press up during a losing session!

If you happen to get hooked on gambling books, I'm sure you'll run across many betting progressions such as 1-2-3-1-2. The first bet is a single unit, then two-units, etc. All these betting progressions are pure foolishness! **In any random game, with a negative expectancy, it makes absolutely no difference over the long term how you vary the size of your bets.** If the casino has a built-in house advantage, it will always prove out, eventually.

It shoots down a lot of interesting theories, but what I've just told you is impeccably true. *You can't change a negative expectancy into a positive expectancy by the way you bet.* Believe it!

But wait a minute! Blackjack has a continually changing expectancy, remember? However, only the few players keeping track of the cards can identify it, and adjust their bets accordingly. If you're not keeping track, then there's little point in varying your bet size.

This is a good place to mention a popular betting recommendation that appears to clash somewhat with our betting rule of maintaining a constant level for non-counters. *Press up when you're winning, and lay back or quit when you're losing.*

On the surface, it seems to make good sense, and it appears to be safe, conservative advice. By pressing up 30% to 50% of your bets when you're ahead, you're betting back some of your winnings, instead of your hard-earned stake, and have actually progressed to a higher betting level without putting yourself in jeopardy. If you're at the right table, at the right time, this advice makes darn good sense!

The only real advantage to pressing up during a win-streak is to insure that you don't miss out on it. But then again, how do you know when it's coming?

The recommendation to lay back or quit when you're losing makes good sense too, right? Indeed it does.

But remember our important rule. *Over the long term, it makes no difference how you vary your betting, unless you're counting the cards.*

Bet Safely

Above all, **never make a bet that you can't afford to lose, or that makes you uncomfortable.** While at the dice tables in Las Vegas recently, I complained to a pit boss that the dice weren't passing. He was a friend of mine so I kidded him a little about how cold the table was, and how much money the casino was making. He said, "Oh, maybe you don't understand, John . . . at midnight, we give all our winnings back to the players, and you have to give back any money that you won too."

Right!

Never lose track of the fact that you're playing with real money. And they won't give it back!

For most beginning players, I strongly recommend that you begin playing for the first time at a $1 table, if you find it. In Las Vegas, try the downtown casinos. On the strip, look for a $2 minimum table. Reno has lots of $1 tables except at the Grand where $2 tables are plentiful. In Atlantic City, $5 and $10 tables are widely in use.

The table minimums are clearly posted on color-coded signs mounted directly on the table. Casinos usually follow the same color-code as their chips. White represents a $1 or $2 minimum. Red is for $5, green is $25, and black means $100. The maximum bets that are allowed vary widely from one casino to another. Generally, $2,000 is the maximum in most casinos, if that's of any significance to you.

The casinos make it difficult for the small bettor to find a $2 minimum table on weekend evenings. I wonder why.

As soon as the casino starts getting busy, all of a sudden the $2 tables become $5 tables, and $5 tables become $25 tables. As in any other business, the casinos know all about "supply and demand."

Don't be forced into playing at a table that requires a larger minimum bet than you want to make. Be disciplined! Try to avoid the weekends if possible, or get up early and try it in the early morning hours. It's a much better time to play. There's less competition among players for the $2 tables, and a more relaxing atmosphere. Besides, chances are you're sharper in the morning, awake and ready to go. Mornings are the only time I play, for all these reasons. Try it!

Tipping At The Tables

In my first book, *Pay the Line,* I recommended that you only tip the dealer *at the end of a playing session,* not during play.

A lot of readers asked, "why wait?" suggesting that if you tip during a good win streak, the dealer will be cheering for you, and hopefully sharing in your profits. It's possible, some readers thought, that a dealer might actually help you win! (Knowing that you are a good tipper.)

And that's precisely the reason why you should not tip while you're playing! Here's an example that should make the point clear.

At the Desert Inn, a few years ago, I sat into a situation at the blackjack tables that probably only happens once in a million hands. A new dealer, as evidenced by her slow, indecisive play and occasional mistakes, had not been properly trained in how to hide her hole-card. My position at the table was "first base," chosen purely at random, but the best spot to see a hole card, if the dealer is particularly sloppy.

As you know, in most casinos the dealer always checks her hole-card when a 10-value or ace is up, to determine if she has a blackjack before the players act on their hands.

To my surprise, everytime this new girl checked her hole-card, she showed it to me. She might as well have stuck the card in my face! It was that blatant. I played a few hands, wondering what the hell to do; continue taking advantage of this incredible situation, move away and avoid the possible confrontation, or tell the pit boss about it. Other players at the table were getting suspicious.

You see, in the great majority of times that a casino is being cheated (especially with a shoe game), it's based on a collusion between a dealer and a player; the dealer in some way clues the player as to a hole-card value. Eye motions, twitches, arm or finger movement. A coded program to get the answer to the player.

Now put yourself in my position. What if a pit boss noticed that the dealer was showing me her hole-card? No doubt the boss would notice that I was winning significantly and tipping the dealer. Do you see that the boss might have thought I had a scam going against the casino, working with the dealer?

Forget it! I don't want to be escorted by a security agent into their interrogation room, and possibly arrested. A little publicity never hurts a gaming author, but not that kind!

I elected to leave the table and later told a pit boss about the condition. I watched him correct the dealer's mistake. He looked over to me and thanked me for calling it to his attention. That table could have lost thousands and any player taking advantage of it, could have been in serious trouble!

Tipping a dealer during play, probably does not encourage any "help" on the dealer's part, but it's possible. The casino's concern is that if very large tips are to be "played" by the dealer, along with the player's bet, it's a temptation they want no part of.

For example, a friend of mine who plays regularly, claims that he can influence the dealer's aid by making large tips. He said that at one time, with large tips out for the dealer, a decision to hit or stand on a stiff would be indicated by the dealer's actions—moving rapidly past the player if the dealer had a potential "bust" hand, or stopping at the player's position and just waiting, a telling signal that the dealer had a "pat" hand.

If you are ever accused of working illegally with a dealer, even though you aren't, the casino won't drag you out in the desert and break your knees. But you might be arrested, if the casino thinks they have a case. At the least, you will be detained, and embarrassed.

For these reasons, I never make a bet for the dealer during play, or tip them at all until the session is over . . . and I'm gone.

I'll tell you about making these bets for the dealers, even though I don't recommend it, so that you know how it works.

Any bet inside the player's betting circle is the player's money, as far as the casino is concerned. Any bet outside the circle and towards the dealer is the dealer's bet. If the hand wins, the dealer's bet is paid off and removed from the table. It can't "ride." Again, for the reasons that the casino doesn't want the dealer to be financially involved with the game to any significant levels.

If the dealer's bet is *inside* the betting circle, then the bet can ride, because the casino considers that bet the property of the player, not of the dealer. It's up to the player to give it to the dealer, at any time, if he so decides.

To be safe, do as I do, tip the dealer only at the end of a playing session, and only if the dealer has been friendly and courteous. Don't tip a rude dealer, regardless of your successes, no more than you would tip a rude, arrogant waitress in a restaurant.

In a recent interview with the Las Vegas Sun, I was asked, "What bothers you the most in casinos?" My quick response was the annoying hustling that sometimes goes on especially from the craps dealers, who beckon the players to make a bet "for the boys." I have an aversion to being hustled, and will leave that table at once. I suggest you do the same. The question was in vogue at the time of the interview as I understand an entire dice crew had been fired from a big strip hotel for hustling the players.

At a dice table recently, my wife was playing with several other women at the table and winning. The dice were really passing. During play, the stickman told the girls, "Hey, how about making a bet for *us*, we're not just here for your fun!"

On that demand, a few girls did indeed make a bet for the dealers, and my wife gave them dirty looks, and left. I wish I had been there. I would have read them the riot act!

This does happen. The player must understand that the dealers are indeed there for the player's fun. It's a sad commentary.

CHAPTER 3

Craps

Dice tables bring out the emotions more than any other game. There's a certain comradery among the players that for some reason doesn't occur as frequently at the other tables. Players feel free to yell, shout, scream, applaud, cheer, and let loose when they're winning. For the seasoned gambler, there are few things in life more exciting than a hot crap table. But it works both ways. Few things are more depressing than a cold table. The dice tables are a roller-coaster ride through the emotions; from sheer exuberance to the depths of despair.

High rollers like to play craps, and contribute to the

game's "electricity" with their large bank-roll. Sometimes, a table can win or lose hundreds of thousands of dollars in just a very short time. That fast! And that exciting!

The casual observer in a casino, who knows little if anything about casino games, would pick craps as the most complicated, difficult-to-learn game. Why? Because the table layout *looks* complicated. There are so many different types of bets. So much confusion. Sometimes 7 wins, and sometimes it loses. Unfortunately, many gamblers shy away from craps because they assume it's too difficult to master.

As any experienced dice player knows, the game is indeed simple. Perhaps the easiest to learn and play. More importantly, it's the most exciting game in the casino. But most important of all, craps offers certain wagers that give the house only a slight advantage. Some of the "best" bets you can make in a casino are at the dice table.

When Atlantic City casinos opened their doors in 1978, the number of craps players surprised even the most experienced casino managers (imported from Nevada). In each casino, the great majority of tables were blackjack, and only a few dice tables were installed. They took their cue from Nevada where a typical casino might have 30 blackjack tables and only six dice tables. In Nevada, that was the right ratio. But not in Atlantic City! The casinos soon realized that craps was a much more popular game in the East, and now the action is considered about even. Some casinos in New Jersey have over 30 dice tables!

How To Play

To understand the game, let's first consider the dice. There are two dice in play, with each cube having six sides, 1 through 6. That means that numbers from 2 through 12 can appear when two dice are thrown.

Let's make an important distinction right now. *The probability of each number varies.* They are not all the same. Your chances of rolling a 4 are much less than rolling a 7. We'll get into that in specific detail later in this chapter, but for now, it's important that you realize this fact from the outset.

Let's list the numbers somewhat out-of-order, so you can best see what the numbers mean for the most common dice wager—the "pass-line" bet. Here are the numbers in groups for you to study. Always think of the numbers exactly as I've separated them.

2-3-12	7-11	4-10	5-9	6-8
Craps	Natural	Point Numbers		
(loser)	(winner)	(must be repeated to win)		

Each of the numbers: 2, 3, and 12 is called a "craps," and it's a loser. 7 and 11 are called a "natural," and it's a winner. The remaining numbers: 4, 5, 6, 8, 9, and 10 are called "point-numbers," and must be *repeated* before a 7 is rolled in order to win.

When a player is handed the dice to throw, the first roll is called a "come-out," and a 7 or 11 immediately wins. The 2, 3, or 12 immediately loses. If the player throws any of the other numbers: 4, 5, 6, 8, 9, or

10 . . . there is no decision yet.

The player continues to throw the dice until either that same point-number is rolled again (in which case the player wins), or until a 7 is rolled (in which case the player loses). Any other number has no significance to the pass-line wager.

Now you can see why the 7 sometimes wins, and sometimes loses. If it's thrown on the first roll, it wins. But if it's thrown while the player is trying to repeat his point-number, the 7 loses. And that's called a "seven-out."

The dice then pass to the next player, and it's his turn to shoot. As long as the shooter continues to make passes (wins), either on the come-out immediately with a 7 or 11, or by repeating the point successfully, he retains the dice. The player keeps the dice even if he loses on the come-out roll with a 2, 3, or 12. *The player only loses the dice when he sevens-out.*

What we've just described is a pass-line bet, the heart of craps, and the most widely made bet at the table.

Now, let's pretend to walk up to the table. Look at the illustration of the table layout. Notice the area marked "Pass-Line." That's where the pass-line wager is made. Place your bet in that part of the pass-line area that's *directly in front of you.*

Also notice that the pass-line extends around both ends of the table. And notice that in fact, *both ends of the table are identical.* For now, don't pay any attention to the rest of the layout.

How do you know if the shooter is "coming-out" or trying to repeat his point-number? It's easy. The first thing to notice on the table is a round 3¾" diameter "puck" that says "ON" on one side, and "OFF" on the

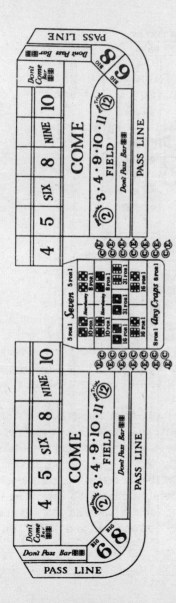

Typical Las Vegas layout, although some newer layouts follow the Atlantic City rule of eliminating the "Big 6 & 8"; a silly bet that pays 1 to 1 if a 6 (or 8) is rolled before a 7. The bet should pay 6 to 5. Even a place bet on 6 or 8 will pay 7 to 6.

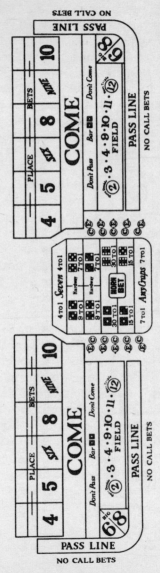

This layout is typical of Northern Nevada casinos. The only major difference between the two layouts is the location of the "don't pass" and "don't come" sections. The Las Vegas layout has a section reserved for "don't come." Northern Nevada combines the two bets in one section.

other. The "ON" side is white, and the "OFF" side is black. Where this puck is located will tell you the stage of the game when you walk up.

Look at the table illustration again, and notice the big boxes at the back of the table that represent point-numbers. There's a set of boxes for both ends of the table. There's a box for the 4, 5, 6, 8, 9, and 10. If the shooter made a point on the come-out roll, and is now trying to repeat that number, that's where the dealers will place the puck. Towards the rear center of the correct box.

When the puck is placed in one of the point boxes, the white side (ON) is up. If the puck is in the box marked "six," that's the point-number the shooter is after.

If the puck is noticed with the black side (OFF) showing, it's usually placed in an adjacent box marked "Don't-Come," and that means the next roll is a come-out.

In Northern Nevada, the don't-come box is in a different spot for some reason, so the puck is placed directly beside (not in) the point box nearest to the end of the table. The puck is nearest to the 4-box on the left side of the table, and nearest to the 10-box on the right side.

As you might imagine, it usually takes more time for a shooter to try and repeat a point-number than to throw a craps or natural on the come-out roll. So, at that instant you walk up to the table, the shooter will probably be going for his point-number. Possibly, you timed it perfectly and the shooter is about to make his come-out roll.

That's your signal to make a pass-line wager. Incidentally, **never make a pass-line bet while the shooter is trying for a point,** because then it's a bad bet. We'll tell you why later in the chapter.

When the shooter wins, everyone on the passline wins! Unlike "street" craps, all the players at the dice table are playing against the house, not each other.

Understanding Odds

The next bet we must learn is called an "odds-bet," and it's directly associated with the pass-line bet that we now know how to make. But before we can understand the odds-bet, we have to learn what "odds" means, and what the correct odds are at a dice table for all the possible numbers. Study the following chart for a moment, and you'll soon learn the probability of rolling any particular number.

NUMBER	WAYS	PROBABILITY	HOW
2	1	35 to 1	1-1
3	2	17 to 1	1-2, 2-1
4	3	11 to 1	2-2, 1-3, 3-1
5	4	8 to 1	1-4, 4-1, 2-3, 3-2
6	5	6.2 to 1	3-3, 2-4, 4-2, 1-5, 5-1,
7	6	5 to 1	1-6, 6-1, 2-5, 5-2, 3-4, 4-3
8	5	6.2 to 1	4-4, 2-6, 6-2, 3-5, 5-3
9	4	8 to 1	3-6, 6-3, 4-5, 5-4
10	3	11 to 1	5-5, 4-6, 6-4
11	2	17 to 1	5-6, 6-5
12	1	35 to 1	6-6
	36		

In this chart, it's readily apparent that there are more ways to roll a 7 than any other number. "Probability" means the same as odds, and it's easy to compute if you have to.

We know there are 36 ways to roll the dice. And we know there are six ways to roll a 7. That means there must be 30 ways to *not* roll a 7 (36 – 6). So our odds of rolling the seven are 30 to 6. Dividing both numbers by 6 gives us 5 to 1.

THE ODDS OF ROLLING A 7:

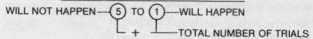

WILL NOT HAPPEN—⑤ TO ①—WILL HAPPEN
+ TOTAL NUMBER OF TRIALS

Out of six rolls, one roll should be a 7; five rolls should be some other number. *That's 5 to 1 odds.* Notice that I said "should be." It's not an absolute. It's an absolute probability.

The actual results may deviate somewhat over the *short term,* and that's what a skilled player is looking for. *An opportunity when the odds have wavered.* But, over the *long term,* a 7 will come up once for every six rolls. Never argue with the laws of probability.

Now that we understand odds at the dice table, let's go back to the pass-line rules and see how we stand. Let's see who has the advantage.

OK, we know there are four ways to throw a craps, and eight ways to make a 7 or 11. Wait a minute! We have an edge here! You bet we do! *The player always has a strong advantage on the come-out roll.*

There must be a catch. And there is. The point-numbers! When the shooter has established a point, the casino gets the edge. Again, it's easy to see why.

There are six ways to make the 7, and remember the 7 loses when a point-number has been established. No other point-number can be made *six* ways. Your best chance of rolling a point-number before a 7 is obviously a 6 or 8, since both numbers can be made *five* ways. But the 7 is more likely.

That's why we said earlier never to make a pass-line bet when the shooter has established a point-number. That's a dumb bet! You're giving up the best part of the pass-line wager—the come-out roll where you have an edge, and you're getting down just at the time when the casino gets the nod. Not too smart!

The next logical question is who has the edge when you take *both* the come-out and point-numbers into account? Not surprisingly, the casino still gets the prize, but not by much. The casino advantage all-total, is 1.41%.

The best way to fully grasp the probabilities of dice is to work out a problem on your own. Let me give you an easy problem to work on, all by yourself, and with the aid of our Probability Chart.

What are the odds that a shooter will throw a point-number on the come-out roll? Your answer will yield an important probability to always remember.

Here's how we find it. We know there are 36 ways to roll the dice, right? And all the ways to throw only a point-number are 24.

POINT NUMBERS	WAYS EACH	TOTAL WAYS
6 & 8	5	10
5 & 9	4	8
4 & 10	3	6
		24

If we subtract the number of ways to make a point-number, 24, from the total ways for all numbers, 36, we have 12 . . . which obviously is the total number of ways *not* to make a point-number. So, 12 to 24 is easily reduced to 1 to 2. That's our answer!

When odds are expressed as 1 to 2, it means that in three trials to make an event happen, one time it won't happen, and two times it will. If we wish to express the odds as a percentage, as is often done, we simply divide the number of times the event *will happen* according to the odds, by the total number of trials (the total of both numbers in the odds expression).

In this case, we divide 2 by 3. That's the fraction 2/3 (fractions are still another way to express probabilities) and a percentage of 66%. *A 66% chance that our shooter will indeed make a point-number on the come-out roll.*

1 TO 2 ODDS EXPRESSED AS A FRACTION, NUMBER, PERCENTAGE:

$$\frac{\text{NUMBER OF TIMES AN EVENT WILL HAPPEN}}{\text{TOTAL NUMBER OF TRIALS*}} = \frac{2}{3} = .666 = 66.6\%$$

*The total of both numbers in the odds expression.

Yet a third way to express a probability, and technically we've already performed it, is with a number between 0 and 1. If an event can't possibly happen, the number is 0. If the event is positively bound to happen, the number is 1. In between are all the decimal numbers such as .666 (nothing more than the fraction expressed as a decimal).

You'll be happy to know that there are no other ways to express a probability that I know of. If there are any,

I don't want to hear about it.

Readers who are learning from "scratch" may accuse me of writing a "trick" question, because the numbers appear to be turned around. Always remember that the first number represents the event *not happening*. Based on the way I purposely phrased the question, the answer of 1 to 2 is correct.

The first number (1), is smaller than the second number (2), because the odds are greater than even (1 to 1) that the event *will* happen.

If the likelihood of the event happening is less than even, as is more often the case, then the odds are obviously expressed with the larger number first.

If the question would have been phrased, "What are the odds that a shooter *will not* throw a point-number on the come-out roll," then the correct answer would have been 2 to 1, because the likelihood of the shooter *not* making a point-number is less than even.

You should now be able to see why we combined the point-numbers in our earlier chart . . . 6&8, 5&9, 4&10. Because the ways are the *same* for both numbers in each pair. Accordingly, when odds are computed for any point-number, it's always the same for the corresponding number in the pair.

Remember the point-numbers in pairs. That's important.

The Odds-Bet

Now that we really understand odds, we can learn how to make the important odds-bet. *This wager is made only when the shooter has established a point.* Place the odds-bet directly behind the pass-line bet, but out of the pass-line area. The casino will allow you to bet an amount equal to your pass-line wager (single-odds) or double the amount of your pass-line bet if double-odds are offered. We'll see later in this chapter that double-odds is a big advantage to the player, so look for the casino that offers it.

What's nice about the odds-bet is that the casino will pay you correct odds on that bet, as opposed to the pass-line wager that pays even money (1 to 1).

Here's a chart that gives you the correct odds of the point-numbers being repeated before a 7 is rolled. It's important that you *remember these odds* because it tells you how you will be paid if you win.

POINT NUMBER	CORRECT ODDS OF REPEATING BEFORE A 7
6-8	6 to 5
5-9	3 to 2
4-10	2 to 1

Let's say the shooter established 4 as his point. If you have $5 bet on the pass-line, you can make an odds-bet of $5 (or $10 at a double-odds table). If the shooter successfully repeats the 4, you will be paid $5, even money, for the pass-line bet of $5, and 2 to 1 for your $5 odds-bet which is $10! (or $20 if you took $10 double-odds).

Since the casino pays off the odds-bet at correct odds, there is absolutely no casino advantage. In fact, the odds-bet is the only bet you can make in the casino that can be determined mathematically to have no advantage either to the player or to the casino. Over the long term, you'll neither win nor lose on your odds-bet wagers.

It's easy to prove that the odds-bet is indeed a fair bet. If the odds are 2 to 1 that a 7 will be rolled before a 4, then the payoff is correct, and the bet yields no advantage to the casino or player. We can compute from the earlier chart in this chapter that there are six ways to roll a 7, and three ways to roll a 4. 6 to 3 reduces to 2 to 1. Since the casino pays off at 2 to 1, they have no advantage.

Logically, you might ask why make such a big deal about a bet that only "evens out" over a long term. Let me answer your question with my own question. Would you rather make bets that *always* give the casino a rock-solid advantage, or would you prefer a bet that's truly a fair game? A bet in the casino that doesn't favor the house, *is* a big deal!

Making the odds-bet along with the pass-line wager reduces the casino's total pass-line advantage from 1.4% to about .85%. Double-odds reduces the house edge even more to about .63%! True, you're risking more money to earn a lower house percentage, but it's strongly recommended.

Although the double-odds bet does not directly affect the house percentage on the pass-line part of the wager, it does lower the percentage for the *total amount of your wager*. And in reality, that's what we're concerned about.

The key to using double-odds sensibly is in the way you "size" your bets. Let's compare a pass-line wager of $15 with no odds to another pass-line bet of $5 with $10 in odds. If the point is 4, you would be paid only $15 in winnings for the $15 pass-line wager, compared to $25 for the $5 pass-line bet with $10 odds. See? It depends on how you structure your bets to earn the advantage of double-odds without increasing your total risk.

Most players have little difficulty understanding single or double-odds, and regularly make the odds-bets as they should.

The problem usually comes in betting the proper amount in order to be paid correctly. Here's an example.

If the player has a $5 line bet and the point-number is 5, it seems perfectly proper to make a $5 odds-bet, right?

Wrong! How can the casino correctly pay off the odds-bet if it wins? 3 to 2 odds means the casino will pay $3 to every $2 wagered. Two goes into $5 two and a half times, multiplied times three is $7.50. A bit elementary but that's the way to think it through.

But, there are no half-dollars at the crap tables! A silver dollar (or $1 chip) is the smallest they have. *Always make sure the payoff is possible for the casino using $1 as the minimum divisible value.*

But what if you only wanted to bet $5 on the line? That's fine. If the point is 5 or 9, the casino will allow you to increase your odds-bet wager to $6. You'll get 3 to 2 for your $6 which correctly pays off a nice $9.00. Incidentally, the dealer will probably give you two red chips (a red chip is $5) and take away one dollar from your original bet.

Of course, with double-odds you would have bet $10 as odds and been paid $15 if the 5 or 9 repeated. Just be sure the correct payoff never includes a fraction of a dollar. And to do that, you have to know what the odds really are.

Look at the chart again. *Think 6 to 5 for 6&8, 3 to 2 for 5&9, and 2 to 1 for the end numbers 4&10.* After a while, you'll know these simple odds as well as you know your own name.

By the way, don't think that payoffs are a problem just with small wagers. A $25 line bet with $25 odds for the points 5 or 9 can't be paid correctly either. You may go to the next unit value which is $30 to insure a correct odds payoff. Odds-bets with 5 or 9 the point, must be divisible by two. Similarly, odds-bets for the points 6 and 8 must be divisible by five. Points 4 and 10 are no problem since they pay 2 to 1. And everything is divisible by one!

Most players unfortunately make these mistakes because they have no inkling what the odds are. If they win, they're happy. *They don't realize they've just been shorted!*

Since the size of your odds-bet seems to be the most confusing issue with new players, let's stay with it for a moment.

The easiest way to make sure your odds-bet can be paid at correct odds, is to play only at a double-odds table, with a red chip ($5) minimum pass-line wager, or any multiple of the red chip . . . two, three, four red chips and so on.

Of course, it also works for a green chip or black chip. Green chips are $25 and black chips are $100, but that's a little steep to start with.

Assuming you begin play with red chips as I do, any odds-bet you make will be double any multiple of $5, and *divisible by both two and five.* It works. Take my word for it.

Incidentally, the casino term for the amount of your pass-line bet is called a "flat" wager. At the double-odds table, simply bet double the amount of your flat wager. It's that simple. You've made the right bet. You've reduced the casino advantage as low as you can. And you know your bet can be paid correctly if you play as most players do, with red chips.

It's a good rule to remember, and a safe betting amount to begin with. Red chips aren't "chopped liver." You can easily work your way up to a total wager of $90 in red chips, $30/$60, accumulate a few "greenies" in your payoffs, and feasibly win over a thousand in just a few rolls.

By the way, never be intimidated by the player next to you who's betting thousands at a crack. There's absolutely nothing wrong with red chips! Pay attention to your own bets, and be content with your "red" action.

Later on, we'll learn how to properly, and safely, press-up your bets as the opportunity arises, but only when you're ahead and winning!

There's only one drawback to what we've just covered, and that's the fact that most casinos only offer *single-odds.* Fortunately, more and more casinos are changing over to double-odds, but what can we do to increase our odds-bet at the *single-odds table*, if that's the only table we can find? Remember that your odds-bet at a single-odds table is usually limited to the amount of your flat wager on the pass-line.

Actually, there are two ways to increase your odds-bet if you're stuck at a single-odds table. And we've already discussed one of them earlier. If you recall, the casino will allow you to increase the odds-bet by a minimum amount to insure that your bet can be paid correctly.

In addition, the casino will also allow you to increase the size of your odds-bet to insure that payoffs will always be in chip values that are the *same or larger* than the value of chips you have wagered on the pass-line.

Here's an example. Suppose your pass-line bet is $30. If you made an odds-bet of $30 and won on a point of 6 or 8, you would be paid $36. Somewhere in there is a silver dollar. If you won on $40, your payoff is $48. A payoff of red, green, and silver dollars.

As a courtesy to the players (that's the casino's reason), they allow the pass-line wager of $30 to $45 to take an odds wager of $50. That's the next multiple of $5 chips that will yield a payoff that can be made *without* silver dollars. Most casinos now use casino-issued silver dollars instead of $1 chips—too expensive to manufacture. The fake silver dollars are usually good in other casinos unlike chips, with the theory they're worth at least a dollar in metal. But don't try to use them back home. The MGM lion doesn't go over as well as Eisenhower at your friendly bank.

To push the point home about making this bet... here's one more example. Say your pass-line bet is $100...four green chips. If the point is 6 or 8, the casino will allow five green chips as the odds-bet. That makes the payoff easy. *Six* green chips to the *five* green chips wagered. No red, all green. Got it?

When I play at a single-odds table, I make it a rule to always bet three chips on the pass-line. Here's why.

The casino will allow an odds-bet of five chips for the

**points 6 and 8, four chips for the points 5 and 9, and a
flat wager of three chips for the points 4 and 10.** That's
especially nice because my winning payoff will always be
nine chips. If the payoff is ever less than nine chips, the
dealer mis-paid me and I won't pick them up until he sees
the discrepency. Dealers do on rare occasion make a
mistake. But not very often. Here's the "three-unit" bet
rule to remember.

POINT	PASS-LINE	ODDS-BET	PAYOFF
6 & 8	3 chips	5 chips	9 chips
5 & 9	3 chips	4 chips	9 chips
4 & 10	3 chips	3 chips	9 chips

The bet is allowed, as we said before, as a courtesy to
the player so that all winning payoffs are in chip values
of your wager (or more, not less). Regardless, it's a way
to increase your odds bet, especially when 6 or 8 is the
point. Three red chips, three green chips, or three black
chips . . . always try to make the three-unit wager at the
single-odds tables.

The Come-Bet

The come-bet is best described as a "delayed" pass-
line wager. And there's no question where to place it. The
largest block of the table is assigned for a come-bet. The
area has the name "COME" boldly displayed.

If you make a come-bet by placing a chip in that area
near your position at the table, it's the same as a pass-
line bet except that you're making the bet *while the*

shooter is trying to repeat a point-number. That's the only time you can make a come-bet, otherwise the bet would obviously be placed on the pass-line since the bet is exactly the same.

Let's say the shooter's number to win on the pass-line has been established as 6. If you wish to have another bet working in addition to the pass-line, simply make a come-bet as I've described. If the next roll is a 9, you'll be looking for another 6 or 9 (before a 7) to win either bet. It can be said that you have two numbers "working" . . . 6 "on the line" and 9 "coming."

Had the next roll been a craps, you would have lost the come-bet. A 7 or 11 would have won outright, but remember, the 7 would have wiped out the pass-line. Mixed emotions!

When a 7 or 11 is rolled on a come-bet, the dealer immediately places the payoff directly beside your bet. It's your responsibility to *immediately* pick up the chips, otherwise the bet "works" on the next roll as another come-bet. On the other hand, if a craps is thrown, the dealer simply picks up your chip, and it's up to you to make another bet.

Assuming the roll is a point-number, your come-bet does not remain in the come area. *The dealer will reposition your bet in the numbered boxes for the point-numbers in a spot that's directly referenced to your location at the table.*

If you're standing at the corner of the table, the come-bet will be moved to the corner of the point-box. That's how the dealer (and you) can keep track of your bets and distinguish them from other come-bets in the same point-box made by other players.

You'll want to make an odds-bet along with your come-bet when it goes to a point-box, for the same reason you must make the odds-bet behind your pass-line wagers when a point is established. Remember, it lowers the casino advantage considerably!

To make an odds-bet in the come area, simply position the bet near the original come-bet and announce to the dealer loudly and clearly, "Odds on my come-bet." Do not place the odds chips on top of your come-bet, for obvious reasons. You recall, I hope, that the odds-bet is paid at correct odds whereby the come-bet (flat wager) is paid only at even money. You *must* keep the chips separate.

When the come-bet and odds-bet are repositioned in the point-box, the dealer places the odds wager on top of the come-bet, but *slightly offset* to distinguish the two different bets. Always watch the dealer to be sure he understood you and in fact, has your bets positioned correctly, and in the proper location.

When the shooter repeats a come-bet point-number for you, the dealer will immediately return your come-bet and odds-bet to the come area where you originally placed them.

Next, he'll place your winning chips directly beside the bet, for you to pick up. Again, if you don't pick up all the chips, they work on the next roll as another come-bet. Be careful!

Incidentally, when you make a come-bet and odds-bet, always be sure to position the bets in the come area *near the perimeter and in direct line with where you're standing.* Don't throw your chips or place them just anywhere in the come area.

Your bet may later be confused with another come-bet placed by another player. It's your responsibility to keep track of your own chips. There's always some jerk at the table who thinks *your* chips are *his* chips.

The best reason I can give you for making come-bets is to gang-up on the table when a shooter is repeating a lot of point-numbers that would otherwise be useless to you. Don't let all those beautiful point-numbers go to waste! That's your cue to make lots and lots of come-bets.

I've seen many instances when a shooter rolled the dice for more than a half-hour before he finally sevened-out. How nice!

You can make as many come-bets as you want to. And when the shooter is throwing numbers, and numbers, and numbers . . . enjoy yourself! Frequently, you might have all five remaining point-numbers covered with come-bets. Quite often, the shooter will roll a point-number that you already have covered with a come-bet.

When this happens, the action is termed "OFF AND ON," meaning the dealer will simply pay your "net" winnings as if the chips moved about on the table as they normally would. Unnecessary actions.

The net result, if you stop and think about it, is that you win the come-bet with odds in the point-box, so that's what the dealer will pay you, directly beside your last come-bet. Pick it up and leave the last come-bet to work again for you. Your original come-bet with odds (on which you were actually paid) will also stay where it is in the point-box, waiting for another *off and on* payoff.

The player may remove his odds-bet wagers any time,

or simply call the bets "off" whenever he likes, on a whim or whatever. Although there's no particularly good reason for doing it.

Of course, the player can't remove a pass-line or come-bet. Otherwise, the player would have a healthy advantage, as we told you earlier by just letting the bet work on the come-out (where the player has a big advantage) and then simply taking the bet down if a point-number is established (where the edge swings to the casino). Obviously, the casino won't go for that!

But, since the odds-bet is fair, no advantage either way, the casino will let you do as you please with it.

They do however, have a standing rule that all odds-bets are automatically *off* on the come-out unless the player says otherwise (that they're working). The theory is that most players don't want to lose the odds-bets in case a 7 is rolled on the come-out which would wipe out all the come-bets placed in the point-boxes. The 7 will in fact wipe out your come-bets, but with the odds called off, the dealer will return all your odds-bets to you. It's a standard house rule, so go with it.

We've just learned the pass-line bet, odds-bet, and come-bet in a manner that may have seemed a bit lengthy to you, especially if you're an experienced player. Sure, I could have reviewed the bets in two or three paragraphs . . . just like the casinos do for you in their little gaming booklets you can get free for the asking.

Purposely, I repeated important aspects of making these bets to help you remember them. Purposely, I went through it slowly with you, using many examples, to make sure you know exactly what to do, and exactly why you're doing it.

This is not a crash course. If you want a succinct explanation of craps, get the free booklet from the casino. But don't look for the bets *not* to make, or any mention of casino percentages. Don't look for fine details as I've given you. You'll learn how to play and you'll learn how to lose. You get what you pay for.

We've spent a lot of time on three particular bets that you can make at a dice table because frankly, **there are no other bets that you really need to know about.** Sure there are lots of other bets to make. But none are as favorable to you as the three bets we've concentrated on. Technically, you should stop right now, review the previous pages, and go play.

I hesitate to tell you about all the other bets you can make at a craps table, for fear you *will* make them. You shouldn't! But to make this chapter complete, here's a brief rundown of all the other bets. Brief indeed, because there's no reason to concentrate on any of them. If you forget them, that's better yet. Here goes.

Other Bets

For the player who's too anxious to get his money on the table, the casino will allow a bettor to "place" any or all of the point-numbers without having to go through the rigamarole of waiting for them to come up as a come-bettor must do.

But for this "luxury," you have to pay a price. Certainly, the casino won't pay correct odds as they do on your odds-bet. No way! Here's a schedule of how the casino pays "place bets." Note the casino advantages compared to .63% on the pass-line and come.

PLACE NUMBER	ODDS PAYOFF	SHOULD BE	CASINO ADVANTAGE
6-8	7 to 6	6 to 5	1.52%
5-9	7 to 5	3 to 2	4%
4-10	9 to 5	2 to 1	6.67%

Granted, placing the 6 or 8 is not that bad, 1.52% to the house. Occasionally, I'll catch myself placing a 6 or 8 if the number's not covered with a come-bet. Still, the casino edge is *two and a half times greater* than a pass-line or come-bet with double-odds. It shouldn't be recommended.

In the event you *do* place a 6 or 8, be sure to make your wager in multiples of six dollars, or six chips, because the payoff is 7 to every 6 you've wagered. For instance, if you bet $30 on the 6, the payoff is $35.

Certainly you can see why placing the 5 or 9 is a poor wager. Indeed, placing the 4 or 10 is totally ludicrous. If you're dead-set on getting immediate action on those numbers, at least "buy" the 4 or 10. That's the next bet to talk about.

For some reason, the casino will give you an option on placing the point-numbers. You can either place them as we've discussed, or you can "buy" them.

If you buy the number, the casino will pay you the correct odds, just like on the odds-bet. But they charge you a 5% commission to do this.

Since the casino edge on the points 5, 9, 6, and 8 is less than 5%, it would be stupid to buy these numbers. But on the points 4 and 10, 5% is obviously lower than 6.67% (the place bet percentage) so it does pay to buy the 4 or 10 instead of placing it.

So, if in your "expert opinion," a whole bunch of 4's and 10's are about to be rolled, go ahead and buy 'em. For every green chip you wager, the dealer will give you two.

I mention the green chip because 5% of $25 is $1.25, but the casino will settle for $1 even. Don't make the buy bet for less than $20 however, because the minimum commission is $1 (the smallest chip at most tables).

Technically, the casino advantage is a little less than 5%, but it's close enough.

Our chapter on craps cannot be finished without a discussion of "prop" bets, but believe me, *you will be finished* if you make them!

Prop is short for "proposition," and that's the name of all these neat little bets you can make in the center layout of the table.

Each prop bet represents a "teardrop" on the casino's chandeliers. Remember that!

The bets are either a one-roll decision or "hardway." If you make a bet on the "hard-six," you win if the number comes up 3-3, and lose if the 6 comes up any *other* way, or with a 7. The accompanying chart details all the prop bets and gives the casino advantages. The heading is appropriate.

DUMBEST BETS AT THE DICE TABLE

BET	PAYS	SHOULD PAY	CASINO ADVANTAGE
Any-7	4 to 1	5 to 1	16.67% (Wow!)
Any Craps	7 to 1	8 to 1	11.1%
11 (or 3)	15 to 1	17 to 1	11.1%
2 (or 12)	30 to 1	35 to 1	13.89%
Hard 6 (or 8)	9 to 1	10 to 1	9.1%
Hard 4 (or 10)	7 to 1	8 to 1	11.1%

On some table layouts, the prop payoffs will be "disguised" as *correct* payoffs such as 8 for 1 on the hard 4 or 10. Sounds like correct odds, right?

Wrong! "For" means you don't keep your bet. "To" does. 8 for 1 is the same as 7 to 1. Don't be misled by the casino's cheap tactic.

The areas of the table layout marked DON'T PASS and DON'T COME are for betting "with" the casino, and against all the other players, assuming they're not all making "don't" bets with you.

If the shooter doesn't make his point, you win, just like the casino. A craps roll on the come-out wins instead of loses, however the casino calls it a "push" on the craps-12. "Push" means no action . . . a standoff.

The casino advantage is about as small as the "right" side (betting the dice *do* pass) and the BAR-12 as the push is called, counts more than you think towards the casino's advantage.

The only problem with the "don't" bets is that you want a cold table to win. You're siding with the enemy.

I never play the "don't" side because it's too damn

boring. No excitement. Which reminds me. Never yell and scream and wave your arms when you win because the shooter sevened-out. Other players may have lost thousands! You'll get "looks that could kill!" Be sure a security guard is handy if you plan on touting your win to the other players.

If you're the type who likes to antagonize other people, the "don't" bets were designed just for you.

A large section of the table layout is devoted to the field bet, and for good reason. The casino makes a healthy profit on field bets, especially on the Vegas "strip" where the house percentage is over 5½%!

The bet wins if any number in the "field" is made *on the next roll*, and losses if any other number appears. Field numbers are 2, 3, 4, 9, 10, 11, and 12. In many "strip" casinos, the bet pays 2 to 1 on the numbers 2 and 12, and 1 to 1 on the other numbers. In Northern Nevada and Downtown Las Vegas, many casinos will pay 3 to 1 for the 2 *or* 12, which effectively lowers the casino advantage to almost 3%. It's still a bad bet, reserved for the player who "thinks" he knows how to play craps. Field bets are the mark of inexperienced, uninformed players.

The Equipment

The game is so basic, that technically we really don't need the table! In the good ol' army days, or in the Bowery, players simply threw the dice against a wall . . . any wall. A building would do, or even a curb. The "table" might have been a sidewalk or a lonely alley. Of course, the casinos won't let you play dice on their sidewalks. That would interfere with valet parking. For the sake of accuracy and organization, the casinos provide tables.

Casino craps tables are elaborate pieces of furniture costing thousands of dollars. In Nevada, there are three different sizes of tables in use, allowing up to 14, 16, and 18 players. The shorter tables are not widely used, although preferred by many experienced players. In Las Vegas, Caesar's Palace uses the short tables, while across the street at the Dunes you can find the longest ones.

At the longer tables, if you're standing at one end and the dice are tossed to the other end, you might need binoculars to read the numbers!

Another problem with the longer tables is the frequency of the dice bouncing off the table. The shooter must bounce the dice off the wall at the opposite end of the table from where he's standing. The longer tables require a longer toss (a harder throw) and "too tall" (off the table) calls are common.

Some players believe that the long tables create problems for the dealers too, especially when the table's full and the dice are passing. There are more players to pay off on each roll of the dice, more confusion, and at the very least, a slow-up of the game.

Personally, I like the short tables at Caesar's so I play there frequently. There's more intimacy around a smaller table and I can see the other end! Incidentally, regardless of the table's size, I always position myself next to the stickman near the center of the table; I never play at a far end. There's a special reason for this rule that many experienced players also heed. *At that position, there are*

four members of the crew that should hear my instruc-
tions: the dealer, the stickman, and both boxmen.
Towards the end of the table, only the dealer is in communication with a player, and any dispute can be difficult
to settle. And there *are* disputes! As impressed as I am
with most dice dealers and their ability to handle pay-offs
with incredible accuracy, occasionally there's a mistake.
And most times, it's a mistake in communication.

Regardless of the table's length, the layouts are all
alike. Having a layout helps to identify each player's bet,
and keeps those bets separate from other players. *It's*
important that a beginning player learns how and where
the dealer positions his bets (those that the player does
not position himself such as the pass-line). Both come-
bets and place bets are positioned in the point boxes
based on the player's relative position around the table.
Here's the way it works. *The front line (side) of each*
point box represents the front row of players, between
the stickman and the corner of the table. *The back line*
of each point box refers to the player's position from the
corner of the table to the dealer (the end sections of the
table). The corner of the table represents the corner of
the point box. Only the front and back sides of the point
boxes are used when positioning your bets.

The longer tables have wider point boxes to allow extra
room for the additional players and their corresponding
bets that might go to the boxes. If in doubt about your
point box position, simply ask the dealer. He'll point it
out exactly for you. And always remember to watch your
bets carefully, especially those in the point boxes. It's
your money!

All craps tables are about 12 to 15 inches deep, creating

a wall that's lined with sponge-rubber shaped in a series of continuous pyramids. That's the reason why the shooter must hit the wall when throwing the dice. To insure a random bounce! In addition, many of the newer tables have a corrogated floor under the felt, to further insure that the dice cannot be controlled.

When I wrote *Pay the Line* a few years ago, I talked to many dice-pit bosses who were familiar with "mechanics." A mechanic is a shooter who tries to manipulate the outcome by his control of the dice. Some of the stories were hard to believe, but allegedly, a few players can indeed affect the frequency of certain numbers and acquire an unethical edge; not necessarily illegal because in some cases, the mechanic uses the wall to deflect the dice at precise angles.

Personally, I doubt the validity of these stories with the possible exception of one fellow who would make his throw in such a way that one dice simply slid along the table's floor (did not rotate) while the other dice tumbled behind it, creating the illusion that both dice were bouncing.

It's interesting, I'll grant you, but don't waste your time even thinking about it. Play the game fairly, and respect the casino's rules.

Casino dice are made of clear, precision-molded, plastic or polycarbonate, to the industry's rigid specifications. The dice are machined square to a tolerance of one ten-thousandth of an inch! The casino is very concerned about the strict consistency of their cubes.

When you play, you'll notice that casino dice have sharp corners, unlike the drug store variety that have radiused (rounded) corners. That's because the sharp corners create more bounce when the dice are rolled.

Incidentally, don't worry about the possibility of a major casino installing "shaved" dice. The casino advantage alone is more than enough to provide a substantial profit. There's no reason for a casino to put their priceless gaming license in jeopardy. Just to be sure, gaming control commissions in Nevada and Atlantic City will inspect casino dice without notice, removing them from any table they choose, then sealing the dice in an envelope for laboratory evaluation. But like I said, casino cheating at craps (or other games for that matter) should be the last of your worries.

The next time you pick up casino dice, look for a confidential code-number the casino uses each day to insure the dice are indeed theirs. Whenever a dice falls to the floor or whenever there's suspicion, the boxman will ask to inspect the dice, noting its condition and code-number.

By the way, the casino refers to a single dice as "dice." The term "die" although correct, isn't used.

The Personnel

Each table is assigned a crew of four dealers, although only three are actually working the table at a given time. The other dealer is on "break." The dealers rotate positions by working 40 minutes "on base" at one of the two ends of the table, then their break, followed by 20 minutes "on the stick." When on base, they are handling the bets of all players at their end of the table. When on the stick, the dealer is in charge of the prop bets at the center of the table, presents the dice to the shooter, and calls the rolls. Since the dealer uses a curved stick to retrieve the dice for the shooter, the term ''stickman'' is commonly used. However, since the player must give instructions to the dealers and the stickman from time to time, it's recommended that the player reads the dealer's name on his breast-badge, and uses it. Don't yell out ''Hey, stickman!'' It's just common courtesy.

The dealers realize that many players are inexperienced, and will be happy to help you and answer any questions.

In addition to the dealers, the casino employs two ''boxmen'' to oversee the game, each being responsible for one end of the table. They are seated at the center area of the table, across from the stickman, and directly over the casino's stash of chips. They watch the payoffs, settle disputes, count bills, and guard the game's integrity by keeping a close watch on the shooter, especially when the dice are in-hand.

The casino arranges its tables in a rectangular configuration (called a pit) and assigns one or two floormen per shift to watch over the group of tables. If any table is hot, and the casino's losing big money, the floormen will give it serious attention, although there's really little they can do.

However, it's not unusual for a floorman to order new dice into a game in the hopes of changing the shooter's luck. And on occasion, they may change the dealer's rotation prematurely, again based more on superstition than common sense. During a really hot shoot, I've seen all four dealers on the stick at the order of the floorman. And on rare occasion, I've seen a nervous floorman pester the shooter. Some of these guys actually feel responsible for the casino's losses.

Floormen also issue markers to credit players, and may on occasion handle some small comps (freebees to high rollers). But for the most part (and this is straight from a floorman) there's not much to do, except keep an eye on the games (and the cocktail waitresses), smoke, and issue a few markers. They have a cushy job, but it can be boring especially when the tables are cold as ice.

Each pit also has a pit boss who's in charge of the entire pit. Big deal. Again, there's not much to do. Occasionally, he'll talk on the telephone (probably his wife telling him to bring home a loaf of bread), also write a marker now and then, and work the computer to check a player's credit balance. But in big casinos, the pit boss has a girl in the pit to do this for him. Obviously, he's too busy with other things.

All the pit bosses report directly to the shift boss (no kidding, another boss) who's in charge of the entire casino for an 8-hour period. This guy generally *is* busy. After all, he's watching the entire casino operation and gets involved with some administrative duties.

Next up the ladder is an assistant casino manager, then the casino manager, and still higher is the vice-president of casino operations. The old adage about chiefs and Indians is perfectly suited for the casino chain-of-command. Too many chiefs, and not enough Indians.

This information is included to help you if you have a dispute or problem in the casino and have not received satisfaction. Get on the phone and ask the operator for the shift boss, if that doesn't work, try the casino manager. Of course, if you still haven't got what you wanted, you can always try the president . . . or the board chairman . . . or the chief executive officer . . . or . . .

How To Bet

I'm constantly asked if I play craps, and if so, how big my bets are—as if the size of my bet is some indication of my skill, or quality of play.

The size of a player's bet has no direct bearing on his ability.

For some players, a large bet is a measure of status. Why would a player want to impress someone by making large wagers? It's not a measure of status; it's a measure of insecurity.

When I play craps, and it's not that frequently, I always begin with a $15 wager, or less if I feel like it. That certainly doesn't qualify me as a high roller! I know that the casino has a long-term advantage, so why take a large risk with a negative expectancy?

The high roller would be bored silly making a $15 bet. He needs the big bet out to feel the excitement, the tingle, the thrill of gambling. In that situation, I can only feel sorry.

I enjoy playing at the table-minimum level because it represents safe, conservative, and smart betting. That's right. **The small bets are the smart bets!**

If I start winning with some consistency, I'll press my bets and might reach the high roller's level, but only after I'm well ahead. Basically, I'm doing what any sensible businessman would do—reinvesting my winnings (earnings) in the hopes of winning larger, future bets. But emphatically, *I'll never risk my original stake by making large bets.* A wise gambler uses only his winnings, but not all of it, in pursuit of greater profits.

Remember to keep your bets small until you start winning. Then, press up 30% to 50% of your bet as you continue to win. *Always put some of your winnings aside to insure that you quit winners.*

Reduce your bets to the table-minimum if you start losing. Quit if it continues. *Never, under any circumstances, press a losing wager.*

A seasoned gambler always follows this classic advice: **Let the winnings run; lay back or walk away when you're losing.**

After a few winning passes at the dice tables, some players who may not have been betting boldly will ask themselves why they didn't bet heavier. Instead of betting only $5, they think what could have happened with $500, or $2,000!

Hindsight is always 20/20. How could you have known when the string of wins was about to occur? Obviously, there isn't any human way, so don't take the chance.

This subject reminds me of the time a few years ago when I was playing in Las Vegas, at a table filled with high rollers. The incident is hard to forget.

Three or four shooters held the dice for quite a long time. The table was red hot! There were lots of big bets out, and the floormen were worried. When the dice finally reached me, I received lots of encouragement from the other players. How could I miss under these conditions?

My first toss was a lousy 3-craps. It lost. OK, no problem. Again, I got more encouragement. "Apologize!" they shouted, "Let's see an eleven!" I threw another craps, two aces. The noise level dropped, and I got some bad stares. Another throw. Craps again! Three losers in a row.

I won't keep you in suspense. I threw two more. That's five craps in a row! But I still had the dice. The next toss was a six. Thank God! At least it wasn't another craps, and besides, a six is easy to make, right? The big bettors made their odds-bets and jumped on all the remaining place bets in an effort to recoup the losses on my come-outs. I made only my odds-bet and grabbed the dice. They bounced hard against the back-wall and came up sixty-one (6-1).

I sevened-out. Six fast losers in a row! It's a good thing it wasn't the "old days" when everyone wore guns!

The story you've just read was nearly edited out of this book. It's really "downer" material. No one wants to hear about six losers in a row, especially when the shooter was the author they're reading. But there are so many lessons in that brief story that it had to be included.

The shooter is incidental to the game's probabilities. The fact that I was the shooter had nothing to do with the outcome. I have no control over the dice, nor do I have any reason to believe that the dice at that time didn't like me.

There's no such thing as a good shooter or a bad shooter. If you see a player at the dice tables who earlier that day had a terrific shoot, don't assume that he'll do it again. He might, but then again, he probably won't. He wasn't skilled. He was lucky. That's all.

Previous rolls have no affect on future rolls. The fact that the shooters before me had such a long success—lots of passes and lots of numbers, had absolutely no bearing on my chances. The dice have no memory.

By the same token, there is no such thing as a number being "overdue." If a shooter has thrown the dice twenty times without a 7 appearing, the dice are not "ready" for a 7 beyond their natural 1 in 6 probability. Do you actually think there's a "force" at work, urging the dice to come up 7? Think about it. The toss of dice will always produce a random event, independent of any previous results.

Winning or losing streaks are real probabilities. The odds of throwing five craps in a row is a staggering 59,048 to 1! Yet it happened. There's a much greater likelihood of throwing five 7's in a row. Any craps is an 8 to 1 probability. Any 7 is only 5 to 1. The player must be aware that, although highly unlikely, streaks of great magnitude will happen, sometime. Hopefully, you'll be there at the right time, not at the wrong time. But remember, you have no way of knowing.

When a winning streak does occur for you, I can only hope that you will have pressed your prior winnings as you should do, and enjoy the ride!

Incidentally, pressing in this book doesn't mean doubling. It simply means increasing the size of your wager by an arbitrary amount up to perhaps 50% of your prior wager.

Learn how to quit winners. Before I "frosted" the dice, many passes were made and I had accumulated sub-

substantial winnings. Even though I had a terrible shoot to follow, *I gave little of it back.* While other players were betting heavily, as if trying to force the wins back again, I bet down. If I had continued chasing the losses, I would have ended up like the high rollers. With nothing.

Table conditions, hot or cold, have no bearing on your expectancy. Let's say that a new player had been able to squeeze in just at the time I got the dice. Knowing the table was "hot," he might have bet heavily. It would have proved disastrous. We know how it turned out.

It's also a good reason why you shouldn't begin a session with a large bet. *Let your actual winnings or losses dictate the size of your wagers.* Don't rely on "playing conditions" because it has no bearing on what you can expect. Technically, there's really no such thing as a hot table. Only a table that *was* hot. At any stage during a streak, no one can say that it's going to continue, but they can tell you how it was.

Remember, there is no scientifically sound reason for a player to worm his way into a "hot" crap table.

Good And Bad Advice

As I mentioned earlier, crap games seem to attract the high rollers, more so than any other casino game, including Baccarat. Individual bets at the baccarat tables might be larger, but the quantity of wagers and the quantity of the big bettors are much greater at the dice tables.

Obviously, high rollers make big bets, and stand to win considerable money when the dice are passing. Their betting habits remind me of what an experienced dice manager in Reno told me about winning a lot of money. He said he has a stock answer whenever anyone asks him how to win lots of money. "If you want to win thousands of dollars you have to bet thousands of dollars." He's partially right.

It's a great way to *lose* thousands of dollars also!

The bottom line on betting at the dice tables is to keep your bets relatively small (unless you're winning consistently) because the casino has the edge on every toss. Remember, the pass-line with full double-odds gives the casino a modest .6% advantage. Come-bets with full double-odds is of course the same percentage, but the place-bets, prop-bets, buy-bets, and field-bets are too much in the casino's favor to consider.

The smart player only makes pass-line and come-bets with full double-odds. That's the mark of a tough player.

If you begin with table-minimum wagers, and progress to larger bets only if you're winning, you represent the toughest opponent possible for the casino.

I don't want to give you the impression that you can make a living playing craps! You can't!

Sure, it's possible that in short-term play you might hit it big. But the more you play, the greater the chance that the casino advantage, no matter how small, will prove itself.

The casinos know that even if a player wins big, it's a temporary set-back. For most players, the game isn't over. The players will probably be back.

Even if you make only the low-percentage bets, there's an important law of probability that applies: *the longer you play, the more likely you will lose.*

Incidentally, hundreds of betting systems are for sale

to craps players, advertised in newspapers and gambling magazines. You must believe me when I tell you that no system can possibly work. *You can't change a negative expectancy into a positive expectancy by the way you bet.*

Betting progressions, as they are commonly called, have absolutely no basis of fact, and appeal only to the gullible, inexperienced player.

Other systems for sale are based on "tracking" the dice looking for numbers that haven't appeared in a given period. By now you should know that it would be a complete waste of time. Yet some people believe in it as the basis for their foolish bets.

Another system that I investigated was nothing more than a course in ESP. Can you believe it?

CHAPTER 4

Slot Machines

A few decades ago, the slot machine was pretty standard. The machines were purely mechanical with no electrical systems. Generally, only a single pay-line was offered, and only a single coin was accepted. Jackpots were measured in the hundreds, not thousands, and certainly not millions of dollars, as they are today.

The modern slot machine has advanced through space-age computer technology to become the casino's most high-tech game. There are several variations in basic machine designs which have become more or less standard in the industry. An astute slot player should learn these basic differences and be able to identify the machine's type, and its method of play.

Today, there are three basic styles of reel-type slot machines: the single pay-line, multiple pay-line, and option-buy. In virtually all cases, the machines are multiple-coin, and it's important that you understand exactly what the additional coins buy for you.

For most *single pay-line* machines, additional coins will simply increase the payoff of any win. The second coin will double the payoff, the third coin will triple the payoff, and so on. Most often, single pay-line machines will accept either 3 or 5 coins. For example, a typical, 3-reel, single pay-line machine accepting up to 5 quarters will have a pay scale for the jackpot of: 200 coins for the first coin inserted, 400 coins for the second coin, 600 coins for the third coin, 800 coins for the fourth coin, and 1,000 coins for the fifth coin.

But some machines that look similar, might pay off the jackpot at lesser values such as: 100 coins for the first coin inserted, 200 coins for the second coin and so on. The player should not immediately think that the first machine is better, because the second machine might include more smaller wins for a greater number of symbols. Perhaps the machine that appears to be better only pays on 7's, bars, and cherries. But the other machine includes additional fruit that could more than make up for the apparent shortage on the big jackpot.

Equally important, some machines offer the jackpot at a higher multiplier for the last coin. For example, this same basic machine we're describing might pay off 2,000 coins on the fifth coin inserted, instead of 1,000 coins. Always be sure to play the maximum number of coins the machine will accept, especially when the jackpot includes this extra bonus!

All single pay-line machines can be easily identified by the words: "ALL PAYS ON CENTERLINE."

For most *multiple pay-line* machines, additional coins will simply increase the number of lines in play *for the same pay scale.* Generally, multiple-line machines are either 3 or 5 lines, accepting either 3 or 5 coins respectively. The first coin inserted into a 3-line machine will activate the centerline. The second coin activates the top line, and the third coin activates the bottom line. With three coins inserted, you have three lines in play. Any winning combination on any of the three lines will pay off.

The 5-line machine is the same as a 3-line machine except that the fourth and fifth coins allow you to play the diagonal lines from the top left of the top line to the bottom right of the bottom line, and from the top right of the top line to the bottom left of the bottom line.

The slot machine usually has a line inscribed on the glass, or a pictorial description on the "feature glass" above the machine, to fully detail the lines that you can play. Most always, the machine's jackpot can only be won on the last line the machine offers (on the third or fifth coin) and sometimes this jackpot is more than the multiple of coins inserted, so always play the maximum number of coins the machine will accept. In other words, play all the lines!

To assure yourself that you have in fact activated all the lines, look for the line to light up on the feature glass above the machine or look for the indication near the actual pay-line. This is important because sometimes the machine will not register your coin-drop. A malfunction is no excuse to the casino. If the line is not lit and the machine does not show that the final coin was accepted, you won't be paid on that line. Period. Be careful. There's nothing more frustrating than to see a winning combination appear on a line that you didn't buy.

The *option-buy* slot machine features a single pay-line and generally accepts 1 to 3 coins. Instead of increasing a payoff or increasing the number of lines, additional coins merely buy the player more symbols to use for winning combinations. For example, a typical machine might offer only cherries as the winning payoffs for the first coin. The second coin will activate bars, and the third coin will activate the jackpot symbols (usually 7's). As always, if you elect to play only one coin, you take the risk of seeing a jackpot total before your eyes without bells ringing and coins dropping. With option-buy machines, always be sure you have all the symbols activated.

The Video Slot Machine

All slot machines today have mechanisms and displays of three primary types: mechanical, microprocessor-controlled mechanical, and video.

The mechanical slot machine was the work-horse through the casino's growth years in the 1960's. Actual reels spinning in their housing controlled by mechanical devices — the way most slot players still prefer. But these "DC-3's" of the casino industry are giving way to the "jumbo jets" — the most sophisticated, secure, esoteric designs that feature CRT video screens, microprocessors, computer logic, and random access generators that can be programmed in any of over 4,000 different modes (percentages).

And to make the whole thing more complicated, the manufacturers today are building mechanical machines with microprocessors inside to control the mechanical reels. Yes, some machines might look mechanical, but in reality they're wolves in sheep's clothing. Inside are the same silicon chips and integrated circuits that drive the video machines.

And that's not all. Some manufacturers are providing casinos with a "kit" if you will, to convert the old mechanicals to the new generation of computer-controlled slots. That favorite old slot you like to play that sounds mechanical today, might buzz and hum tomorrow. Expect to see many mechanical machines in your favorite casino with the guts of a computer. That's an important issue when our discussion of percentages comes up later in this chapter.

Video slot machines are easy to recognize. A 13″ television screen provides a simulation of spinning reels, creates a lot of cute noises, and displays cute little phrases on the screen like... "I'm loose as a goose!" Experienced slot players, for the most part, don't like video machines, but that's another matter. In the years ahead, it will be interesting to see if the manufacturers, the casinos, or the players determine the slot machine's destiny. Will the mechanicals fade away? Will all slots be video?

Since most gamblers are cynical, somewhat distrusting of machines they don't understand, the reluctance to accept this new generation of slots is understandable.

Some players are concerned about the incredible complexity of video machines, and the underlying fear of high-tech manipulation. For the old-timers, the change alone is what's upsetting. Was there anything really wrong with the good ol' mechanicals?

Slot machine manufacturers have tried every trick in the book to make the video machines look like and feel like the real thing. Some machines actually show the reels backing up when you begin to pull the handle, just like a real slot machine. Others provide the sounds of the reels "clicking" into position. Still others are attempting to put the mechanical "feel" into the video handle.

Despite the fact that many players prefer the mechanical machines, most casino executives and slot machine manufacturers contend that the video machine represents the future. In most any other business, the old adage about giving the customer what the customer wants holds true. In this case, however, it looks like a "force play" is about to ensue.

The most important issue here however is the "fairness" aspect of the video machine, not the conjecture of its place in the future. Any concern that the video machine could easily cheat the player is unfounded. In consideration of who's operating the machines, and the casino license on the wall, cheating the player is an inconceivable enemy. Especially in the case of the major casino-hotels, the player stands a more likely chance of falling out of an airplane.

Remember that most all casinos can generate substantial income honestly. There's absolutely no reason to cheat. The only instance I can think of involving a slot cheating scam against the player, with the knowledge of management, happened years ago in Northern Nevada. Upon discovery, the Nevada Gaming Commission revoked the casino's license and the operation was completely shut down.

Perhaps the deciding factor in the video slot's future is the positive aspect of its accuracy and reportability to the casino. All video machines, and the microprocessor-controlled mechanicals, are usually connected to a central computer, providing immediate reports on the machine's performance, activity, and condition.

The casino will know instantly if there's a malfunction, an undesirable performance in terms of the set percentage, and for that matter, exactly how the machine has profited for the casino in terms of handle (all bets), hold (the casino's winnings), and percentage. More so, the casino can tell if the machine has been altered, opened, tampered, or tilted. If the machine has been opened, the computer will identify the pass-card holder (a magnetic card is required for access) and monitor the machine closely while open and vulnerable. If a jackpot hits, the computer will alert the casino instantly, and later determine if the jackpot was legitimate.

As you can see, the computer-controlled slot machines are a friend to both the casino and the player.

As the new generation of slot player emerges, raised on video arcades and electronic games, the battle between the mechanicals and the videos will be more or less academic. For the seasoned slot player however, it appears the microprocessor-controlled "mechanical" machines we talked about earlier will be their only saving grace.

The Jackpot

Perhaps the most significant variation among slot machines is the jackpot. Again, there are three basic types: standard (non-progressive), double individual progressive, and multiple-progressive.

The *standard* machine pays a fixed jackpot amount that is clearly posted on the feature-glass of the machine. Most often, the standard jackpots are stated in the number of coins to be won. Sometimes a dollar amount is given. If you're playing a quarter machine with a jackpot of "1,000," be sure you know whether you're playing for 1,000 coins ($250) or a thousand dollars!

The standard machine generally provides a more realistic chance for the player to win the jackpot. Accordingly, the jackpots are not as huge as the ones you read about in the papers. Nonetheless, we'll learn later in this chapter that playing these fixed jackpot machines might be a better move for the player than the million-dollar progressives. The player's odds of winning a jackpot has to be considered in determining which machine to play. Although odds of 8,000 to 1 seem high, such odds are considerably more realistic than 8,000,000 to 1! Later on we'll see how your chances of winning the really big jackpots should be considered as a "hold" percentage against you, along with the casino's normal hold percentage that represents their profit.

Of course, if you're the type of player who can't get excited about the chances of winning a $200 jackpot, your greed is going to cost you dearly. A successful casino player, whether at the slots or at the blackjack tables, must learn how to be happy with a win of any amount. Winning always beats losing, and frankly, winning at all in the casino today is not that easy. Be thankful.

In order to provide larger jackpots, playing on the gambler's greed, the casinos have developed the popular *double individual progressive* machine that pays an ever-increasing jackpot amount depending on the amount of play. The jackpot might reach high proportions in comparison with the same machine without the progressive jackpot feature.

The term "individual" means that the escalating jackpot is based solely on activity of that particular machine, and not affected by other machines nearby. As more and more coins are pumped into the machine, the progressive jackpot increases by a small, fixed amount per wager. The jackpot continues to grow until a lucky player lines up the right combination.

The term "double" means that the machine offers two distinct jackpots, both displayed on a lighted meter at the top of the machine. Usually, a red arrow will signal the jackpot amount that is in effect for each handle pull. The arrow alternates between jackpots with each coin inserted. Most progressive machines in the casino that operate individually have double jackpots.

It's common sense for the player to look for individual progressives with the highest jackpot totals (on both meters), since the *amount* of the jackpots has no bearing on the percentage of hold. As in all cases, the casino's percentage of hold is always based on the probabilities of a machine over a long-term, averaged period, *inclusive of the jackpots* that probably will occur based on the odds of that event happening over tens of thousands, maybe hundreds of thousands of trials. The casino relies on the law of averages. It hasn't failed them yet.

Sometimes progressive machines are "banked" together in what the casino calls a "carousel." Unlike the individual progressives, the carousel of machines all contribute to a single progressive meter, brightly displayed above the carousel for everyone to see. These special machines are called *multiple-progressive,* and provide the slot player with a chance to win hundreds of thousands, even millions of dollars. The temptation of a "7-figure" jackpot is hard to resist.

Surprising to most players, these machines give the casino their biggest profits, in spite of the huge payoffs.

There's much confusion over the percentages of these high-paying progressives, and most players assume that the casino must hold a high percentage in order to pay off the big jackpot winner. But it isn't so. You must understand that the casino does not pay the jackpot out of their hold percentages (profit). If the casino's hold on the million-dollar progressives is 10% (a likely number), then over a long term of play the casino will have made 10% of all coins inserted as profit, *after* the big jackpot has been awarded! The casino's actual hold takes into account all jackpots, including the biggie.

A popular notion among frequent slot players is to avoid the million-dollar progressives because... "you have to pay too much." In a sense, that's right. But let's look at *who* you're paying.

A common practice in many casinos with the big-money carousels is to remove 10% of the handle (all money wagered) each day and place this money in an escrow account. The casino is not saving the money for themselves; it's certainly not their profit! The casino is in fact saving the money for the ultimate winner! This 10% escrow hold has nothing to do with the casino's regular hold percentage that we've estimated for this example to be 10%. In addition to the 10% "hold" in escrow for the eventual winner, the casino continues to earn it's regular 10% "profit" hold.

So, the player in reality is faced with a 20% hold against him assuming that he won't win the ultimate jackpot — which for all intents and purposes is a logical assumption. The odds are almost beyond comprehension!

Getting back to the notion we quoted, ". . . avoid the million-dollar progressives because you have to pay too much," let's finish that statement. You have to pay too much to the casino, *and* to the ultimate winner! It's your money, and all the other player's money, that pay the big winner. The casino doesn't pay the winner, you do. All of you do.

Technically, it's not entirely fair (mathematically) to "revise" the hold percentage of these machines taking into account the 10% or so of the handle that goes to the winner, and considering it as a hold against all the players. Together, that 10% along with the casino's profit percentage of 10% totals 20%, and that's not the least bit attractive.

But in the case of the giant jackpots, it *should be* revised because your chances of winning the jackpot are slim and none. It's a virtual certainty that you won't make it. For the other machines with more sensible jack-pots and far better odds of winning, then we must consider that jackpot as a real probability for us, and weigh only the casino's actual hold against us.

Incidentally, the casino makes big profits on million-dollar carousels not because they turn up the percentages, but because these machines receive so much play. Heavy action! Regardless of the actual percentages against us — and it might be better than 10%, maybe 5% or even 3%, the casinos are the consistent winners.

Another interesting facet of the big progressive jackpots is the short-term unpredictability of winning it. You'll recall that short-term play can result in wide fluctuations from what the true probabilities call for. It's true for the player, but it's also true for the casino! Two or three big wins within a short time-frame, however remote, might raise havoc in the casino's accounting department. If such wins did occur before the casino was able to set aside a substantial escrow, then the casino might indeed pay the winners from their own earnings.

Another factor that the casino worries about is the initial vulnerability after a jackpot has been awarded, depending on the amount the casino sets on the meter to begin the next jackpot. In some cases, the casino might actually be taking some mathematical risk.

More Variations To Look For

All video machines are either reel slots, poker, black-jack, or keno. Technically, when a player refers to a video slot, he's talking about the reel-type, not one of the other games. Most likely, the distinction is because the video slot has a handle. And all slots are suppose to have handles, not buttons. Most slot players refer to video poker machines as ... well, poker machines, not slots.

We've already discussed video slots, and will devote an entire chapter to poker machines. There's little doubt among the experts that poker machines have become the fastest growing casino game. And there's a lot to be said about them.

The "21" machines (blackjack) are also relatively popular, allowing the inexperienced blackjack player to cut his teeth against a machine instead of a real dealer. The rules are basically the same as with the live game, but of course the betting is limited and the excitement is not nearly the same as at the tables.

Video keno has not received the same degree of acceptance, and accordingly will not be detailed in this text.

There are still two major types of machine variations that we haven't yet covered. For one, all slots accept different coin values. In most casinos, you'll find either 5^c, 10^c, 25^c, 50^c, and $1 machines. Of these values, the 25^c and $1 machines are by far the most popular.

Slot machines, whether video or mechanical, offer an array of symbols that usually relate to the size of the payoff. The smallest jackpots are generally cherries, followed by the other fruits: lemons, plums, oranges, and watermelons. Bells and stars indicate moderate payoffs generally, and represent the oldest symbols on the machines. The higher payoffs including jackpots are usually reserved for bars, 7's, or the casino's logo. If the machine uses bars in the payoff scale, generally single bars are lowest, double bars are next, followed by triple bars for the largest jackpot. In some cases, a machine will offer a payoff for any combination of bars: single, double, or triple.

Understanding Odds

The percentages associated with all slot machines are based on what the manufacturers call reel-strips. Although the video machines are based on the same principle, it's easier to understand the concept of "programming" percentages if we consider the mechanical machine with actual reels inside.

As you know, most slot machines feature either 3, 4, or 5 reels. And each reel has a position at which the machine will stop.

Now we have the ingredients to determine the frequency of payouts — *the number of reels and the number of stops per reel*. It's really that simple.

The best way to grasp the probabilities of different stops on the reel lining up with identical stops on another reel is to use a coin-flip as an example. Let's say we want to find out the odds of "heads" coming up three times in a row.

First, we have to determine the number of all possible outcomes (probabilities). And to do this, all we need to perform is a simple calculation of multiplying the number of probabilities for each trial, times the number of probabilities for the next trial, times the number of probabilities for the next trial, and so on.

For all you mathematical geniuses out there, you can see that if the number of probabilities is the same for each trial, we simply raise the number by the power of the number of trials (an exponent).

In the case of the coin-flip, there are obviously only two probabilities for each trial — heads or tails.

So, in the case of three coin-flips (three trials), the total number of probabilities is: $2 \times 2 \times 2 = 8$. Eight different ways that the coin will come up in three trials. Since we know that heads will come up three times in a row only once out of these eight probabilities, the odds of doing it should be expressed as 7 to 1. Not 8 to 1. The first number in our odds expression represents the number of times the event won't happen. The second number represents the number of times it will. The total of both numbers is the total number of all possibilities.

If you're a football bettor, and you guess at the selections like we all do, your chances of winning three out of three games is 7 to 1. Not so good! Surprised?

OK, we're not going to the casino to flip coins or bet football games. Let's get back to the slots.

If there are 20 different stops on the first reel of a 3-reel machine, you can be assured there will be 20 on the second reel, and 20 on the third reel. If it just so happens that only *one* "7" (our jackpot symbol) appears on each reel, what are the odds of hitting that jackpot?

Simply multiply $20 \times 20 \times 20 = 8,000$. There are 8,000 different combinations that can come up, but only one combination is our 7-7-7. So the odds are: 7,999 to 1. And if you think that's bad ...

With 4 reels, it's a staggering 159,999 to 1! With 5 reels, (are you sitting down?) it's 3,199,999 to 1!

To really comprehend the severity of these odds, let's compare the chances of hitting the 5-reel, 20-stop machine to getting struck by lightning. The odds are about the same! Now, if it just so happens that in the course of your lifetime, you've been struck not once but twice, I suggest you hurry off to Las Vegas, find a casino, and get some change. See if you're really that lucky. But don't stand under a Palm tree!

In order for casinos to offer large jackpots, in the hundreds of thousands of dollars, it's necessary to make the odds of hitting that jackpot even more remote.

So, to accommodate the casino's demand, the slot machine manufacturers have developed reels with more stops — 22 and sometimes 25 per reel. If you really want to know the odds on a 5-reel machine with 25 stops, it's 9,765,624 to 1.

But you must realize that the odds have to be that great in order to provide the chance for a super-jackpot. There has to be that kind of relationship between the odds and the jackpot amount. Otherwise, the casino simply couldn't afford it.

In the case of the video machines which are based on reels and stops that really don't exist, a microprocessor stores all the information necessary to simulate the reels and stops. Since it's all done on a "chip," the programmers can produce as many as 255 stops per reel. I'm not even going to bother figuring out the odds.

Until recently, most video slots were limited to 84 stops per reel, so to increase the odds for a giant jackpot, only the number of reels could be increased.

But today, slot machine manufacturers can utilize a new chip that provides an incredible 255 stops per reel! So, if you see an easy-looking 3-reel machine with an unusually high jackpot, forget 84 and think 255. Think 255 x 255 x 255, and then consider another machine.

Let's get back to earth by discussing briefly the smaller

payouts, like cherries. On a basic 20-stop, 3-reel machine, there might be 7 cherries on the first reel, 7 cherries on the second reel, and 4 cherries on the third reel. The odds of lining up 3 cherries is: $7 \times 7 \times 4 = 196$ chances of appearing out of 8,000 combinations = 7,804 to 196 = 40 to 1.

I can live with those odds! Out of 41 pulls, you should receive one three-cherry payoff. But don't expect a million dollars. In line with the odds, you'll receive a modest payoff at best.

Understanding Percentages

The slot manufacturers "adjust" the percentage of a machine by considering all the possible combinations and all the possible payouts including the jackpot. If you play the machine one coin at a time for 8,000 plays, and if the game was fair (no advantage for casino or player), you should expect to receive back 8,000 coins in winnings.

But of course the game isn't fair, and the machine will probably not give you back the full 8,000 coins, at least not over long-term play. The number of coins the machine holds divided by the total number of possible combinations represents the casino's percentage (the advantage against you). If, for example, the machine was set to return 7,200 coins over 8,000 pulls, the casino will hold 800 coins. 800 divided by 8,000 is 10%. And that's the casino's advantage — 10%.

The slot manufacturers have two ways to set the percentage. They can design the reel-strips as they please with any arbitrary number of symbols, and they can adjust the pay-scale that you see displayed on the machine's glass. **The frequency of symbols on the reel-strip, number of stops, number of reels, and the schedule of payouts, *together* control the machine's percentage.**

Usually, each stop on a reel-strip is represented by a symbol; a cherry, lemon, bars, or whatever. But in some cases, the stop position might have no symbol at all. Stops that are void of any symbol are called "ghosts." Today, you'll find many of these machines in the casino, although a lot of players don't like them. Generally, ghost machines have fewer pay combinations, but they are generally larger. A ghost machine is not necessarily a higher percentage than the others, contrary to popular belief. The "ghost" feature has no bearing on the percentages, so don't hesitate to play it for that reason.

Invariably, a slot machine's percentage is established at the factory based on the instructions of the casino as noted on their purchase order. *Forget the notion that a casino can adjust a screw or turn a hidden knob to change the percentages.* Mechanical machines require a great deal of work to change a percentage, and the newer video machines require a skilled technician. Most often, the casino knows what they want and what they are doing beforehand; rarely is a change required after installation.

The slot machine industry uses a term to describe the success of any machine — "attract mode." It is this factor based on "player appeal" and the equally important term, "stay mode," that determines if a machine has found its home. Percentages are rarely changed to make a machine more popular. The machine must have some "commercial" attraction to lure the player, and a relatively satisfactory payout to retain the player. Indeed, slot machines today are more attractive than ever before, with cosmetic consideration as if designed on Madison Avenue. You'll find bright, lively colors, flashing lights, audio gimmicks, and video messages that beckon the passers-by. Today's slot machines are as hard to resist as ever.

Identifying The Percentages

When talking about percentages, the casino refers to it as "hold." And so shall we. **In Atlantic City, the New Jersey Casino Control Commission has established regulations that require all casinos to return at least 83% to the player.** Simple arithmetic tells us that the hold percentage must be 17% or better. So, if the hold is indeed 17%, **over the long term** you can expect to lose $17 for every $100 you risk.

In Nevada however, there is no regulation that specifies a minimum return to the player or maximum hold percentage for the casino. Technically, Nevada casinos are free to set the percentages of their machines as they please. The Nevada Gaming Commission does require however that all slot machines have a jackpot of any stated amount that can be won. If the machine doesn't have a payout of some value, then it's not considered a gambling device and couldn't be approved for use. How nice. At least you know you won't be face to face with a machine that never pays out.

Well, as it turns out, the spirit of free competition accomplishes the same thing as stringent regulations. In order to survive in such a competitive marketplace as

Nevada, the casinos generally provide "decent" hold percentages. It doesn't take long for players to become suspicious of high percentages, and when the word gets out, that greedy casino will be as lonely as the Maytag repairman.

Although there are no sure ways to determine a reel-slot's actual percentage, I strongly recommend that you *monitor your own play* to determine the percentage as best you can.

Begin with a determined amount of money and let your winnings accumulate in the coin-tray. Play only your original stake, not your winnings! Then, when your initial money is gone, count your winnings. You can easily tell if your "win" is 90%, or 80% or hopefully 120% or more of your original money. You'll be checking frequently over short-term play where, as you know, the fluctuations can be significant. Always keep a record. If the percentage appears to be too steep, move on, or quit.

Always look for advertised hold percentages on the casino's marquee or in newspaper ads in the local papers. If a casino is promoting 97% return on slots, go for it. When you get inside, if you find that the slot machines identified as 97% turn out to be only eight to ten machines, and all being played, then leave at once. Don't let the casino "bait and switch" you! Your guess on the other machines is as good as mine. Stay away!

In the next chapter, we'll learn that poker machines, unlike reel-slots, offer the player a chance to literally shop for percentages. The player can base the percentages on the feature-glass pay schedule right on the machine, and not worry about what's inside!

CHAPTER 5

Video Poker

Video poker machines were first introduced to the gaming public in 1976, receiving a rather luke-warm reception. Although Bally Manufacturing Co. gets credit for the initial debut, International Game Technology (IGT) entered the market in 1978 with resounding success, and deserves the lion's share of the credit for pioneering the machine's acceptance. Today, poker machines are taking more and more floor space in the casino, receiving play from over 25% of all slot players, according to a visitor's profile-study commissioned by the Las Vegas Convention and Visitors Authority. That percentage is expected to increase dramatically over the next few years. The report also indicated that 10% of all visitors played poker machines. That figure is more than keno, more than roulette, and even exceeds craps! There's no doubt about it. Video poker machines are a huge success story!

According to the manufacturers, poker machines have gained in popularity because of the skill element involved. As you know, there is no skill associated with conventional reel-type slot machines . . . only luck. With poker, the player has decisions to make. Decisions that can greatly affect his chances of winning.

And there's another important reason for the poker machine's widespread acceptance. It's a proven fact that a great many people like to play poker, but are intimidated by the casino's poker parlors. Some people do not wish to join in at a live game against players they don't know. The poker machine is just that . . . a machine. No intimidation. No apprehension. No strangers. And of course, there are no "tells" to read, and no bluffs to worry about. It's poker, but at the player's own pace, in the player's own world.

How To Play

To review the game, the basic rules of poker apply. The "rank of hands" is the same.

The machines are based on a popular poker game called "5-card draw," affording the player an option of drawing up to 5 additional cards. If you're not familiar with draw poker, it's simple.

When you insert your coins, five cards will appear on

the 13″ color screen. In order to make the best poker hand, you may discard up to five cards and receive that number in new cards which will appear on the screen to make your final hand. If you have a hand that earns a payoff, the machine will do so automatically.

There is no handle to pull; only buttons to push. Since most machines take from 1 to 5 coins, the machine will not display the first five cards until the 5th coin is inserted. If you elect to play less than 5 coins (not recommended), you must "tell" the machine to "deal" (push DEAL button) since it obviously doesn't know if you're just slow putting in the rest of the coins, or if in fact you are finished betting.

After the five cards appear on your screen, you are now faced with an interesting decision. Which cards will you discard, if any, and which cards should you hold? After making your decision, you simply push the "hold" button that corresponds to each card you wish to keep, and then push the "draw" button. The machine will give you a new card in the place of the ones you discarded. Now, the machine will determine if you have a winning hand, and if so, the machine will pay you according to a pay-scale shown on the machine's feature glass. If you don't have a winning hand, which happens 55% of the time, the machine will simply wait for you to play your next coins.

Incidentally, if you receive a winning hand on the first five cards, such as a straight, flush, four-of-a-kind, or straight flush, be sure to push the hold button for all five cards. Then push "draw" (although you will not receive more cards) to tell the machine you are keeping the initial hand, and get ready for a nice payoff.

RANK OF POKER HANDS
(IN ASCENDING VALUE)

HAND	DESCRIPTION
Jacks-or-Better	Any pair of Jacks, Queens, Kings or Aces.
Two Pair	Two pairs of equal value cards such as two 3's and two 10's.
Three-of-a-Kind	Any three cards of the same value such as three Queens.
Straight	Any five cards in *consecutive* value, not of the same suit, such as 4 of clubs, 5 of hearts, 6 and 7 of spades, and 8 of diamonds.
Flush	Any five cards of the same suit, such as 8, 10, Jack, King, and ace of hearts.
Full House	Five cards that include a pair and three-of-a-kind, such as a pair of Kings and three 10's.
Four-of-a-Kind	Any four cards of the same value (all four cards of the four different suits) such as the 8 of hearts, diamonds, spades, and clubs.
Straight Flush	Any five cards in consecutive value, *of the same suit*, such as 2, 3, 4, 5, and 6 of diamonds.
Royal Flush	*Only* the 10, Jack, Queen, King, and ace *of the same suit*.

To discuss all the possible player strategies for all the possible hands would be somewhat beyond the scope of this beginner's text, however, it should be made clear to the reader that the large jackpot for a royal flush should always be considered a primary goal, and to that end, the player may find that a draw decision clashes somewhat with basic poker strategies. For example, if your hand is Jack, Queen, King of hearts, 10 of spades, and 10 of diamonds, you must discard the pair and go for the royal flush.

Of course, common sense has to apply here also. If your hand is 10 of hearts, 10 of diamonds, 10 of spades, 10 of clubs, and Jack of clubs, don't throw away your four-of-a-kind trying for a royal flush with your 10-Jack of clubs. Use your head! You have plenty of time to think. The machine won't rush you.

Be especially careful with straights. They are rarely arranged in ascending or descending order, and might be hard to notice. Remember that the ace counts as either high or low in making the straight.

Since virtually all machines pay a 4,000 coin special jackpot for a royal flush with 5 coins inserted (compared to 250 coins for one coin inserted), it behooves the player to insert all five coins. For all other wins, additional coins increase the jackpot by a linear progression — four-of-a-kind pays 25 coins for the first coin, 50 coins for the second coin, 75 coins for the third coin, and so on. But the royal flush pays more than this natural progression for the fifth coin, and accordingly, weighs heavily in the player's overall expectancy. Although the chances of making a royal flush are about 40,000 to 1, these odds should not be considered "out of the realm" especially when compared to the ridiculous millions to 1 odds that the player faces at some reel-type machines.

How To Determine The Percentage

What sets poker machines apart from the other reel-type slots is much more than just "player skill." **Perhaps the most important aspect of poker machines is the ability of the player to judge the percentages by a simple review of the pay-scale clearly outlined on all machines.**

Unlike the conventional slot machine, where percentages are hidden in the reel-strips and among over 4,000 programs, poker machines have the same basic "insides" and only a few different pay-scales to rate.

All poker machines are based on a regular 52 card deck, shuffled after 30 to 40 cards are played (some machines shuffle after each deal), so you can correctly assume there are no hidden differences to be worried about, at least not that I'm aware of.

Keeping track of specific cards, as you might do in a live poker game, is not of value to the video poker player because of the automatic and unpredictable shuffling.

To ascertain the machine's percentage of hold, the player only needs to review the pay-scale and look for the most advantageous payouts. Here's a chart that shows four of the popular pay-scales. Notice how significant the percentages change depending on whether or not the machine returns the player's bet (even money) on jacks-or-better.

POPULAR VIDEO POKER PAYTABLES

		COINS PAID OUT							PERCENTAGE	
JKs	2PR	3K	ST	FL	FH	4K	SF	RF	W/JKs	W/O JKs
0	1	3	5	6	9	25	50	250	—	66-68%
1	2	3	4	5	6	25	50	250	92-94%	73-75%
1	2	3	4	5	8	25	50	250	93-95%	74-76%
1	2	3	4	6	9	25	50	250	96-98%	76-78%

Shown here are four of the more than 50 paytables available, that the player is likely to see in the casino. Note the importance of whether or not the machine pays on Jacks-or-better, nearly 20%! This chart is based on the first coin inserted. 5th coin/royal flush pays 4,000 coins.

From this chart, it can be concluded that the best chance for the player lies with the machine that pays 6 coins for a flush, and 9 coins for a full house. Be sure, however, that 2 pair pays 2 coins. **Indeed, you must be sure that "jacks-or-better" returns your bet!**

Although it's a break even proposition, you should make jacks-or-better over 20% of the time. The casino's advantage goes up over 20% without this important feature. Always look for it!

Player's Skill

Another factor in determining the actual percentage is the degree of player's skill. The percentages found in this chapter are based on average player decisions. Of course, a player could make poor decisions, throwing away straights, breaking up a flush, holding the wrong pair, etc., and could theoretically give the casino a huge advantage. In this case, our pay-scale percentages go out the window.

At the other end however, a player could conceivably achieve a high level of skill and make the right decisions perhaps 99% of the time. In this case (according to Bally), the best pay-scale percentage of 98% could be cut even lower to "98.778%." We're getting "picky" numbers, but at least it's moving in the right direction!

Since some poker machines feature big progressive jackpots, some authors contend that if the jackpot is large enough, the machine's percentage might actually favor the player! Technically, that might be true, but it's a dangerous notion.

If you are confident that the progressive jackpot is a mathematical certainty in your favor, and you wish to risk literally thousands of coins in pursuit, you must be prepared to lose it all. THERE IS NO GUARANTEE THAT IF YOU WAGER 40,000 TIMES, OR EVEN 100,000 TIMES, THAT YOU WILL LINE UP THE ROYAL FLUSH. NO GUARANTEE WHATSO-EVER!

Assuming that in fact you will not make the royal flush, even though it's much "easier" than the million-dollar slot progressives, the poker machine will keep over 4% for the house based on the most favorable pay-scale for the player. That's why we said earlier that the big jackpot counts heavily towards the minimal casino advantage. But you have to win it at least once over the full course of all probabilities, and that's a hell of a lot of coins!

Unlike the conventional reel-type progressives, the royal flush jackpot is indeed realistic and should be counted when considering percentages. All I want to make sure you understand is that although 40,000 to 1 is better than 3 million to 1, it's still a major hurdle to clear. It could take a big investment. But then again, it might not.

That's what gambling is all about.

Cash-Less Slots

This is as good a place as any to discuss a new trend in slot machines, including video poker, called "credit-play." Instead of dumping your payoff in the metal coin-tray, a machine might simply hold your winnings until you decide to take them by pushing the "cash-out" button. The problem with this feature is that too many players don't push the cash-out button. They simply play off the credit meter until it shows "0."

It would appear to be better for the player to actually see and feel the coins in your tray to fully appreciate the value of the coins, as opposed to the meter that only displays a number. This problem is analogous to credit at the table games. A player simply asks for a marker and plays it. No cash. Just a piece of paper. In too many cases, credit in the casino is a loaded gun.

Remember, the number of coins displayed on a credit-meter is *your* money, not the machine's money. Take it!

There's another new concept in slot machines under-way that will allow the player to use a credit card, instead of actual coins.

The player will apply for the casino-issued credit card at the cashier's cage, and deposit money to play against.

To play, you will simply insert the card into the machine, and immediately see on the screen your balance and record of activity. Each time you play and lose, the machine will debit your account. When you win, the machine will credit your account.

Eventually, it's possible that you can use your Master-Card or Visa card to play a slot machine. What next!

CHAPTER 6

Roulette

Roulette is an easy game to determine mathematically. Although this isn't the right time to study the wheel in mathematical terms, it's important to realize from the outset that mathematically it can't be beaten over the long term. In other words, "luck" isn't going to make it.

If we consider the wheel a symmetrically perfect device, able to produce purely random numbers, we might as well stop right now. Roulette has a built-in mathematical advantage for the house that simply won't budge.

Like I said, a study of all the possible outcomes, odds,

and probabilities of roulette will lead you to a chilling mathematical conclusion. The game ain't fair!

Along the same lines as trying to beat the wheel with luck—that we called the "mathematical" assault, is perhaps the most time-tested of them all . . . *systems*. Since day-one, even the most astute mathematicians have tried countless, esoteric systems of picking the numbers or making the wagers. None of them have ever worked. None of them ever will.

There are several systems widely popularized based on picking the number, color, or odd/even factor that is based strictly on previous numbers. Keeping track of the wheel's decisions with pencil and paper is a complete waste of time. It should be elementary, but needs to be said . . . **the wheel has no memory**. Previous numbers have no effect on future outcomes.

If red has come up five times in a row, the next spin will yield no more or no less a chance for red to come up again, regardless of the scoreboard. The odds are the same every time the little white ball drops. This, my friend, you must believe.

Since there are 38 compartments on the American "Double Zero" wheel—18 red, 18 black, and two green—the odds are easy to compute. There are 38 probabilities all total. And we know there are 18 ways to make red. So, the correct odds of winning on red are 10 to 9. Here's how we get it.

The first number in an odds expression represents the number of times an event will *not* happen. The second number in the expression represents the number of times it will. The total of both numbers in the correct odds expression is the total number of all probabilities, win or lose.

If there are 38 probabilities total, and we know that there are 18 probabilities that will win, the difference is obviously the number of probabilities that will lose—20. So, the odds are 20 to 18, reduced to 10 to 9. Expressed as a percentage against you it's 1/19 (one net loss out of 19 trials) or 5.26%.

Similarly, the many systems being touted that deal with betting progressions are equally useless and deserve little space here. It's important that you realize that no method of varying your bets will change the expectancy. It makes absolutely no difference, *over the long term*, how you vary your bet size. If you wish to challenge me on that statement, go play. At some point in time, the wheel will have taken every cent you have.

Now we know all the ways that you can't beat a roulette wheel. You can't beat it mathematically. Luck is no factor. Tracking the numbers is a sucker's system. And foolish betting progressions are for losers.

I purposely put the two "losing" assaults first, and left the best for last. Now, let's look at two assaults that seem to make sense, and might have some merit.

The "Wheel Bias" Assault

The idea of a roulette wheel having some sort of bias is not new, but represents the basis for some new, interesting theories.

Over the years, gaming authors have contended that a roulette wheel cannot be perfectly symmetrical, cannot be in perfect balance, and cannot have precisely the same compartments. Technically, it has to be true. Nothing in this world is perfect . . . except my mother-in-law.

The roulette wheel is indeed precision-machined and constructed. Every effort is made to insure a random distribution of numbers by eliminating any potential bias. But there are so many wheels in operation; can they all be perfect? Isn't it possible that at least a few are defective? Isn't it possible that over the years, a particular wheel has developed a bias through constant use? Of course it is. It's not only possible, but probable.

But how does one go about finding a biased wheel? The casino certainly isn't going to hang up a sign over a particular wheel saying "This wheel is out of wack!" On the contrary, the casino inspects each wheel frequently by "skilled technicians" looking for any signs of unusual wear. Dealers must report to the manager whenever they suspect a particular wheel is biased toward a certain segment or side. And it does happen!

To the player's favor, I have serious doubts about the casino's routine inspection. And I'm a little leery of the casino's "skilled technicians." I want to meet one of these guys sometime and see what kind of sophisticated equipment he uses.

For the player who is serious about winning, I strongly recommend that you record the activity of a particular wheel before you play. Don't confuse this recommendation with "system" play. You'll be looking for a bias. You'll have sound reasoning for performing your "tests."

If a particular segment of the wheel seems to be getting the most action, by all means play it! But be careful!

It could be a bias, but then again, it could be just the un-predictable pattern that occurs from time to time in random numbers. But it might not! And that's the point. Depending on the frequency of your tests . . . and your patience, the results might yield a distinct advantage for you.

Players who are looking for wheel bias can usually be identified by their method of playing a certain segment of the wheel, not a particular number. No bias could be *that* bad. Divide the wheel into approximate quarters or eighths. After you've logged a substantial number of decisions, see if any segment of the wheel is producing more than the natural probabilities for that grouping. Remember, the odds of any one number hitting are 37 to 1. For three numbers, it's 35 to 3; for 8 numbers, it 30 to 8 (15 to 4) and so on.

Looking for wheel bias is no easy task! But it can be fun. And assuming you're not betting the farm while you log all the numbers, it shouldn't cost you one penny. It's the cheapest form of casino entertainment I know of.*

Incidentally, don't expect to measure any bias, if there is any, with only a few minutes of watching. Get serious. Most often, players who are dead-set on finding any bias employ a "team" concept. One member works the wheel for the first hour, the second member for the next hour,

---

*If you are interested in the "wheel bias" concept, I recommend that you read Allan Wilson's *The Casino Gambler's Guide* (Harper & Row), 1970. Wilson devotes a lengthy chapter to this fascinating subject.

His book is one of my favorites. In spite of its copyright date, it remains an excellent value for today's player.

and so on. At the end of the period, sometimes days and days, they all gather to compare their data. Of course, there's usually some indication along the way whether or not the effort looks fruitful.

In some cases, casinos have been known to switch wheels on unsuspecting players, and totally destroy all their research. What a crummy deal! If you are beating the wheel through a detected bias, you can expect a casino countermeasure. The wheel switch is the most common ploy.

The "Wheel Clocking" Assault

OK, so the idea of standing around a roulette wheel for days on end doesn't excite you. Sure, looking for wheel bias can be downright boring, based on a game that's basically boring anyhow. Only a select few players can really get into it.

But clocking the wheel is a different story. We're not looking for a defect in the wheel, we're looking for a hint as to where the ball will fall, based on three important factors: *the speed of the wheel, the speed of the ball, and the relative position of the ball and the wheel at a particular time.* Does it sound complicated? It really isn't, especially after we analyze it.

Players who believe in clocking a roulette wheel harbor strong feelings about the wheel's inability to produce unpredictable random numbers. Remember, we're not talking about a defect in the wheel itself, but in the design . . . the original concept!

Unlike the keno hopper, where "ping-pong" balls are

so thoroughly mixed, and then so randomly selected, the roulette ball might be somewhat predictable based on a calculation of speed and its relationship to the wheel.

Similarly, dice at the craps tables bounce, roll, and rebound with totally unpredictable results. But the only significant "interference" at the roulette wheel that's of any concern to our clocking concept are the few deflectors (canoes) that are placed along the sloping vertical wall to deflect the ball as its momentum decreases.

My personal opinion is that the clockers have a valid argument about the wheel's value as a nonprophetic random number generator. Later, we'll study the clocking concept in greater detail, giving you my own personal assault (it's not a system) that works along these same lines, but focuses more on the roulette dealer's uncanny and unintentional tendency to spin the ball (and the wheel) at remarkably similar speeds, time and time again.

Since the dealers spin the ball so many times each day and every week, they tend to develop a "programmed" motion, much like we all try to do swinging a golf club, or rolling a bowling ball. Their "delivery" seems to be "grooved," especially if they've been doing it for a long time.

Clocking the wheel, and my way—clocking the dealer, have strong possibilities that we must consider.

A few expert roulette players who are proficient at clocking the wheel have devised elaborate devices built with microprocessors to judge the speed of the ball and the wheel, compute the relationship between the ball and the wheel position, then instantly determine a most likely section of the wheel where the ball will drop.

This sort of ammunition for the player will make

roulette more exciting, and give the game a shot in the arm like the computer strategies have done for blackjack. Unfortunately, the casinos are reacting much the same as they did in the 1960's when the new blackjack strategies were revealed. They're fighting back.

In 1985, Nevada Governor Richard Bryan signed into law a bill that makes it unlawful for any person to use or possess any device to assist in projecting the outcome of a game. So much for clocking a roulette wheel right? Well, not really. Only "devices" are outlawed. We can still use our brains. I still think there's a way to legally and ethically clock the wheel, using the device between our ears. And we'll get to that in more detail later in this chapter.

How To Play

There are eleven different kinds of bets that you can make at a roulette table: a single number; two, three, four, five, six, or twelve-number groups; a column of twelve numbers; the color red or black; whether the number is odd or even; and whether the number is from 1 to 18, or 19 to 36.

Of all these bets, only the single number wager is of interest to the wheel-clocker. Of course, the bet can't be for just any one number; that would be too hard to pinpoint. Usually, a wheel-clocker will select a group of six to eight numbers, all adjacent on the wheel, and make a single-number wager on each number.

The wheel itself has 38 numbered compartments: the numbers 1 through 36, plus two green "numbers," 0 and

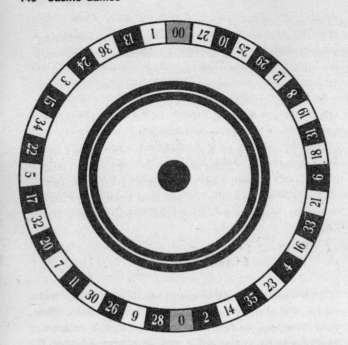

00. Eighteen of the numbers are black, and eighteen of the numbers are red. If the green numbers were not on the wheel, the player would have a 50-50 chance (1 to 1 odds) that the ball lands in a black (or in a red) compartment.

The wheel is carefully laid out so that red and black compartments alternate, except at the green "00" position where both "1" and "27" are otherwise adjacent, and at the green "0" position where both "28" and "2" are otherwise together. More so, a pair of even numbers alternates with a pair of odd numbers, except near the green positions.

The only other "intelligent" aspect of the numbering format is the placing of an odd number on the wheel with the next highest even number directly opposite, and in different colors. For example, "2" is directly opposite "1," and "4" is directly across from "3."

The ball is controlled by the dealer, who propels it around a track at the upper section of the wheel's housing. It's interesting to note that the wheel spins in a counter-clockwise direction, while the ball spins clockwise. The wheel itself weighs over 100 pounds and thereby creates a fly-wheel effect that keeps it spinning at a minimum speed for a surprisingly long period. Furthermore, the wheel is point-balanced for minimum friction. The dealer only occasionally has to give it a boost.

As the ball's speed diminishes, it leaves the track and comes to rest in one of the 38 compartments. Along the way, a series of deflectors in the shape of a "canoe" will catch the ball and help to promote a random result. Some wheels have eight such obstacles, while some of the newer versions have sixteen, equally spaced around the wheel's housing. Deflectors provide the main threat to a wheel-clocker.

Each compartment, all precisely the same size and shape, is formed with metal partitions (called frets) that also tend to deflect the ball as it seeks its final resting spot.

Most players assume the ball is made of precision-machined ivory, and it was until recently. Now, the little white ball is made of precision-machined plastic. Either not enough elephants, or too many pianos.

The roulette wheel is positioned at the far end of a long

table which also includes the betting layout. The dealer stands between the wheel and the betting layout, while up to six players are seated around the area of the table where the betting layout is located.

Many authors suggest that certain seats are better than others in terms of visibility of the layout and convenience in making the wagers. But wheel-clockers are not interested in *any* seat. They stand. Remember, the wheel-clockers aren't just guessing at the numbers like the other less-fortunate players at the table. They are paying close attention to the wheel, the speed, and the relative position of the ball and the wheel at the time the speeds are computed. Accordingly, they must stand close to the wheel; and then be ready in an instant to reach over the players who might be in their way and place their favored bets.

The rule on making bets at the roulette table is a bit loose, but generally, you are not allowed to bet after the dealer has called "no more bets," at a time when the ball is just about to drop from its track. Some dealers might rush the call a little, and some dealers might let you push the limit.

Unlike the conventional roulette player who usually makes his bets before the ball spins, the wheel-clocker must first watch the wheel and the ball, make a decision, and then place his bet. Most casinos alert roulette dealers to be on the watch for this type of player. If the alleged wheel-clocker is winning consistently, or presents a threat to the casino, the floorman in charge of the pit will keep a constant eye on the player and might harrass him a little. At that time, the smart wheel-clocker calls it a day or visits another casino, aware that his "skill" has been noticed.

Making bets at the roulette table is a bit different from any other casino game. In fact, roulette is the only game where the player does not have his own personal spot to place bets. The layout provides only one area for each bet for all the players. If all bets were made with regular-issue casino chips, you can be assured there would be mass confusion. Even Henry Kissinger couldn't straighten it out.

Accordingly, each player's chips must be distinguishable from the other players, and to do this, the casino provides up to seven different colors of chips—a different color for each player.

When you wish to buy roulette chips, the dealer will ask what denomination you desire for the value of each chip. Until you tell him, the roulette chips have no value whatsoever. Once determined, the dealer will place a "marker" button, showing the correct chip value, on your supply of chips located behind the wheel. In addition, some casinos will place a chip of your color directly on the wheel's rim along with an additional marker button on top, to avoid any later confusion or dispute.

All casinos have minimum chip values and minimum bet sizes, that vary widely from one casino to another. In addition, there are maximum bet limits, usually $500 or less. Today, many casinos use 25 cents as the minimum chip value, and some require a $1 or $2 minimum wager.

In addition, the casino usually wants you to buy at least 20 chips, called a "stack." I can't honestly tell you why, but it's a long-established rule, so go with it. Give the dealer $20 and you'll receive 20 $1 chips, or 40 50-cent chips, whatever value you want them.

Remember, the chips have a value only at the roulette wheel, and only at that time that you're playing. *Never leave the roulette wheel with roulette chips in your pocket.* You'll be stuck if you do. It's an important aspect of the game to always remember.

Incidentally, if the table is not busy (as is usually the case), most dealers won't mind if you wager with regular casino chips, provided no other player is doing the same. And many casinos will let you wager real money, and pay off in casino chips. But always check with the dealer first, to learn the rules in effect at that particular time.

All bets at the roulette wheel are divided into two categories: "inside" and "outside" bets.

Inside bets are made by placing your chip (or stack of chips as one wager) on a single number, or at certain locations on the layout (actually on the lines of the boxes) to signify a group of numbers from two to six.

Any inside bet must meet the table minimum, however the casino will allow multiple bets of less than the table minimum provided they total the table minimum or more. In some casinos, a relatively small maximum wager is posted, such as $25 maximum on inside numbers. The casino's theory on this restricted maximum bet is based on the high payoff odds for inside betting. A player on an incredible win streak could possibly "hurt" the casino with exceptionally large bets. That's the casino's answer. Personally, with such high maximum wagers at the craps tables on the high-odds proposition bets, and at the baccarat tables where maximum limits are often raised to $6,000 or more, I believe it makes little sense to restrict the roulette limits, unless of course, the casino questions the predictability of their

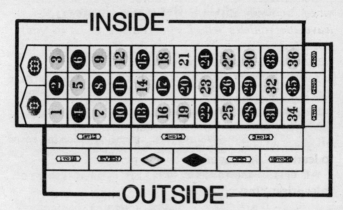

own game.

Always check before you play to be sure you understand the betting limits, especially if you're playing in different casinos.

Outside bets are made by placing your chips in the sections shown that identify the wagers paying 2 to 1, or 1 to 1 odds. The casinos usually allow a much higher maximum bet for the outside wagers, but *each* bet requires at least the table minimum.

When payoffs are made, the dealer first removes all losing wagers. Next, the dealer pays off all outside bets, but leaves the bet (and the payoff) in the respective betting area. Finally, the dealer computes the winning payoffs in the inside betting area and slides the payoffs to the winning player. However, the dealer leaves the original wager in the same betting area. So, it's important that you pick up your chips after each winning bet, unless you wish to press the bet (provided it's under the table maximum), otherwise the bet will indeed work on the next spin, whether you wanted it to or not. Be careful.

Straight-Up Bet (One Number)

A straight-up bet is simply a bet on a single number. On our sample layout, we've shown a straight-up bet on the numbers 14, 29, and 0. Since there are 38 different compartments on the wheel, there are a total of 38 different straight-up bets that you can make.

Like all bets, the straight-up wager wins or loses on the next spin of the wheel. And, you can wager on as many different numbers as you like.

Be sure that you place your chip completely inside the boxed number. Don't touch a line because that will denote a different type of bet that we'll cover next.

A straight-up bet pays 35 to 1.

Split Bet (Two Numbers)

A split bet is made by placing your chip on the line, any line, that separates two adjacent numbers on the layout.

A split bet gives you two numbers that are working for you on the next spin of the wheel. If either number hits, you win!

On our illustration, we've indicated three split bets: the numbers 4 and 5; 16 and 19; and 0 and 1.

There are 62 different ways to make a split bet.

A split bet pays 17 to 1.

Street Bet (Three Numbers)

A street bet gives you three different numbers with just one wager. The bet is made by placing your chip as shown on our layout, on the line that separates the inside and outside betting area, giving you that particular row of three numbers. In addition, you can make a street bet on the 0-1-2, 0-2-00, and 2-00-3 as shown on our chart.

There are 15 possible combinations of three-number wagers you can make.

A street bet pays 11 to 1.

Corner Bet (Four Numbers)

A corner bet is one of the most popular bets at the roulette table, but don't ask me why.

The chip must be placed at the junction of four numbers. We've indicated two different 4-number bets on the layout: 20-21-23-24; and 1-2-4-5.

There are 22 possible corner bets that you can make.

A corner bet pays 8 to 1 odds.

Five-Number Bet (Five Numbers)

This bet is the only one that is not recommended, because the house advantage is greater than the game's otherwise consistent 5.26%.

There's no particular reason to make this bet, so let's not spend much time on it. Forget it.

The five-number bet pays 6 to 1.

Line Bet (Six Numbers)

Here's a relatively unpopular bet that provides the player with six numbers for a single wager. Think of it as a "double" street bet, where you have two adjacent streets of numbers.

This bet must be placed between two rows of three numbers, on the line at the left of the inside layout.

There are 11 ways to make a six-number line bet.

The line bet pays off at 5 to 1 odds.

Column Bet (Twelve Numbers)

The column bet is an outside wager that allows the player to cover 12 numbers, representing one of the three vertical columns of a dozen numbers.

On our sample illustration, we've shown the column at the far right, beginning with 3 and ending with 36. Most column players prefer this row because the numbers in the column are easy to remember: the common multiples of 3 beginning with 3 . . . 3-6-9-12-15 etc.

There are obviously three different ways to make a column bet. **Column bets pay 2 to 1 odds.**

Dozen Bet (Twelve Numbers)

This bet is another way of covering 12 numbers, but unlike the column bet, the numbers are in numerical order: 1 through 12; 13 through 24; and 25 through 36.

Your wager should be placed in the outside section indicating the 1st 12, 2nd 12, or 3rd 12. The dozen bet represents another popular wager that a lot of players prefer.

On our sample layout, we've indicated a dozen bet for the middle third, 13 through 24.

The dozen bet pays 2 to 1 odds.

Red Or Black (18 Numbers)

This is the bet that most novice players like to make, and for many players is the essence of the game. You have the best likelihood of winning as compared to the inside wagers, but the odds payoff is greatly reduced to even money.

The diamonds at the far left center of the betting layout are in black and red, and indicate the position for making this wager.

A red or black bet pays 1 to 1 odds.

Odd Or Even (18 Numbers)

This bet is similar to the red or black wager we just described, except you're betting on whether the number that wins is an odd number or an even number. Like red or black, you have only two choices. It can't be that tough.

The boxes for making this bet are easily identified.

An odd or even bet pays 1 to 1 odds.

1-18 Or 19-36 Bet (18 Numbers)

This bet is another even money proposition, whereby you're guessing whether the winning number will be low or high.

Again, the correct box for making the wager is obvious.

Of the three even money wagers, this bet is the least popular.

The 1-18 or 19-36 bet pays 1 to 1 odds.

Improving The Odds

So far in this text, all discussions about roulette have been in reference to the "double zero" wheel with both the green "0" and "00." But some casinos in both Nevada and Atlantic City have experimented from time to time with the "European style" single zero wheel, in the hopes of attracting more players. The single zero wheel has only one green spot, for a total of 37 positions as compared to 38 with the extra "00." **Since the single zero wheel pays off at the same odds as the double zero wheel, the house percentage is effectively reduced to 2.70%!** The player will lose, according to the probabilities, one unit out of 37 trials. 1/37 is 2.70%. As you recall, with the double zero wheel, the player should lose two units out of 38 or 5.26%. The European single zero wheel is hard to find, but for the serious roulette player, it's certainly worth the effort.

As of this writing in August 1985, only a few casinos in Nevada, very few, offer the more attractive version. Surprisingly, several casinos in Atlantic City now offer the single zero wheel, but generally require a much higher minimum bet. Since casinos are notorious for changing their rules frequently, it would be of little value to publish the names of the casinos now offering the single zero wheel.

Besides the possibility of finding a single zero wheel, casinos in Atlantic City offer the roulette player another big advantage.

If you're playing a double-zero wheel, and betting on any of the 1 to 1 payoff wagers: red/black, odd/even, or 1-18/19-36, the casino will only remove one-half of your bet if the ball lands in a green compartment. This action is termed "surrender." The net result to the player is one unit in losses over 38 trials, or a reduced house percentage of 2.63%!

Until recently, Atlantic City casinos offered an option for the player whereby the European "en prison" rule could be substituted for the ½ bet loss, although the net result is the same for the player. "En prison" means that if the ball lands on a green spot, there is no decision on any bets with 1 to 1 payoffs. The player's bet is placed "in prison" until the next spin of the wheel. Then, if the right number hits, the bet is "removed from prison" (but isn't paid). It's then up to the player to either make the bet again, or remove it from the table. In 1980, the Casino Control Commission dropped the "en prison" feature but left the "surrender" option available.

The "en prison" feature or the surrender rule at a single zero game, if available, will greatly reduce the house advantage to a low 1.35% as represented by a net loss factor of ½ unit in 37 trials. In this situation, roulette, even by simple mathematical standards, is an attractive game! But try to find it. In the great majority of cases, you'll be facing two green compartments (double zero wheel) without the benefit of "en prison" or "surrender." Then, we're back to the 5.26% house advantage which can make slot machines look good!

As you might have already guessed, surrender is not presently offered on single zero wheels in Atlantic City, however, there are some indications that it might be considered in the future to perk up the game. Indeed it should!

Many casinos in Europe and other parts of the world continue to offer en prison on their single zero wheels, so we've included the percentages for this feature on the chart that follows on the next page. Remember, either surrender or en prison cuts the house percentage in half for the 1 to 1 bets.

The Mathematics Of Roulette

If the casino pays off your winning wager with an amount that's something less than the true probability of winning that bet, then they have acquired an advantage over you.

As you can see by the chart on the following page, all wagers are paid off at certain odds that are less than the correct odds of winning.

For example, a split bet pays $17 to a $1 wager, but should pay $18. Remember that the total of both numbers in a correct odds expression represents all the possible outcomes (probabilities). So in the case of our split bet, the total number of probabilities is 19 (18 + 1). To find the house advantage, all we have to do is divide the number of units (dollars, in this case) that we will lose by the total number of probabilities. If the casino pays us $17 but should have paid $18, we are short $1 (our loss). $1 divided by 19 is .0526 or 5.26 cents lost out of each dollar. As a percentage, simply move the decimal two places to the right (just like we did to get cents) and we have 5.26%. That's the casino's advantage, and it applies on each and every spin.

A careful look at our chart shows us that playing the

ROULETTE PAYOFF TABLES			DOUBLE ZERO		SINGLE ZERO	
TYPE OF WAGER	NUMBERS COVERED	ACTUAL PAYOFF	CORRECT ODDS	HOUSE EDGE	CORRECT ODDS	HOUSE EDGE
Straight-Up	1	35:1	37:1	5.26	36:1	2.70
Split	2	17:1	18:1	5.26	17.5:1	2.70
Street	3	11:1	11.7:1	5.26	11.3:1	2.70
Corner	4	8:1	8.5:1	5.26	8.25:1	2.70
Five-Number	5	6:1	6.6:1	7.89	Not Available	
Line	6	5:1	5.3:1	5.26	5.17:1	2.70
Column	12	2:1	2.2:1	5.26	2.1:1	2.70
Dozen	12	2:1	2.2:1	5.26	2.1:1	2.70
Red/Black	18	1:1	1.1:1 (1.05:1)	5.26 (2.63)	1.05:1 (1.03:1)	2.70 (1.35)
Odd/Even	18	1:1	1.1:1 (1.05:1)	5.26 (2.63)	1.05:1 (1.03:1)	2.70 (1.35)
1-18/19-36	18	1:1	1.1:1 (1.05:1)	5.26 (2.63)	1.05:1 (1.03:1)	2.70 (1.35)

The numbers in parentheses represent the odds or house edge for either surrender or en prison that some casinos permit on the 1:1 payoff wagers.

double zero wheel with surrender (in Atlantic City) is almost the same advantage to us as playing a single zero wheel (without surrender). The difference is only .07%!

Confirming that surrender at the double zero wheel yields 2.63% for the 1:1 payoff bets is easy to do. Again, we know there are 38 total probabilities. 18 of our numbers will win one unit, and 18 numbers will lose one unit. Two numbers (both green) will each lose 1/2 unit. So, in 38 trials, we should lose a total of 1 unit (1/2 + 1/2). 1/38 equals 2.63%.

At the single zero wheel, these same 1:1 payoff bets also gives us one losing unit, but out of only 37 probabilities (37 compartments). And 1/37 equals 2.70%.

The only mathematical part of roulette that many players can't understand relates to the payoff for the split bet and all the other multiple-number inside bets. For example, most players know that the actual payoff for a straight-up bet (one number) is 35 to 1. Since a split bet is for two numbers, it would appear that the correct payoff for a split bet should be half as much as for one number, one-half of 35 to 1, or 17½ to 1. But the casino only pays 17 to 1 for a winning split bet. It looks like the casino has shorted you another one-half unit.

Actually, 17 to 1 is the correct payoff and yields the same house percentage as a straight-up bet because the casino will not take the half of your wager that represents the losing number of your two-number bet.

Confused? OK, let's try it again. If you're making a $2 wager on a split bet of numbers 4 and 7, and number 4 hits, the casino will pay you $34 for your winning number, and leave all of your original bet on the table for you.

Technically, 1/2 of your $2 bet won, and 1/2 lost. But the casino considers the bet as either a win or a loss. If either number hits, it's a win. Since the casino does not take the half of your wager that lost, it makes up for the apparent discrepancy.

A $2 split bet will yield the same payoff as two straight-up bets for $1 each on the same numbers. Remember, your $2 split bet wins $34. If you would have wagered $1 on each of the numbers 4 and 7, you would have won $35 for the winning number 4, and lost the other $1 for the losing number 7. See, you yield a net win of $34 either way. Got it?

What The Casinos Say

In downtown Las Vegas, the El Cortez gets a fair amount of action, according to 11-year shift boss, Wayne Starker. He indicated to me that the casino had experimented with single zero wheels from time to time, but returned to the double zero game because the "new" game didn't get much more action. If you recall from our previous discussions, the single zero wheel cuts the house percentage from 5.26% to 2.70%. But not enough players appreciated the change. Starker thinks that a lot of players didn't realize the difference in the percentages, and for that matter, might not have even realized that the wheels were any different at all!

This same account had been related to me by several other casino managers which certainly doesn't say very much for roulette players. According to Paul Burst, director of casino operations for the Claridge Hotel in

Atlantic City, they too tried the single zero wheel and soon realized that ". . . the action was pretty much the same. The small increase in the drop was not enough to justify the lower hold." Incidentally, the term "drop" means all the cash and credit slips that are dropped into the slot of the table and into a metal holding bin. The "hold" represents the casino's percentage; a more literal term for the money the casino makes as their advantage in all the games.

At the Sands in Las Vegas, casino manager Doug DuCharme can recall a single zero wheel when he first started there a few years ago. Of course, the wheel is long gone, and you can pretty much guess why.

Some of the hotels I talked to that do offer the single zero wheel, generally require a higher minimum bet. Instead of a dollar or two, the minimum bet might be as high as $25. So, either the player doesn't know what he's looking for, or does . . . but when he finds it, he can't afford it!

Regarding wheel-clockers, Starker told me that he sees players at the El Cortez with stop-watches and calculators quite frequently. But according to a guy who should know, he says they lose at the same rate as anyone else. As a lot of casino managers told me, "gadgets" at the roulette wheel are commonplace.

Atlantic City has a law much like Nevada that prohibits a player from using an electronic or mechanical device such as a calculator or computer that assists in projecting the outcome of a game, or analyzing the changing probabilities or playing strategies at any table game.

Some casino managers appeared to be sensitive about

"devices" and some indicated that they were only mildly concerned.

Much of the concern is at the blackjack tables and directed primarily to card-counters. In the case of roulette, as based on my findings, it would appear you could drag in a mainframe computer, plug in some strobe lights, send the data to NASA, and hold an MIT seminar at the same time . . . without raising an eyebrow.

Well, maybe not. Don't take me serious. Devices are risky, and regardless of some casino's liberal policy, are blatantly unethical.

In talking with the casino managers, there was no question where they draw the line. **Past-posting!** This is the most common cheating scam at the roulette tables, and one of the casino's biggest sources of aggravation. A cheater will cleverly sneak a bet on the layout *after* the ball has dropped in a pocket. Sure, it's a great way to pick winners, and it's a great reason to need an attorney. The casinos will prosecute!

According to DuCharme at the Sands, past-posters usually work in teams; one or two members will distract the dealer, while another member actually places the bet. Most often, past-posting is on straight-up bets where the payoffs are 35 to 1. In a short time, the casino can suffer large losses. DuCharme says that on weekends, or whenever busy, it's the practice of most casinos to employ a "mucker," another dealer who stands at the far end of the table and watches only the layout. Otherwise, it's difficult for a single dealer to spot a past-poster with all the action from so many players.

Besides clocking the wheel, I asked about the little known tactic of clocking the dealer—looking for identical, systematic patterns in the way the dealer spins the wheel and the ball.

DuCharme was quick to point out that his dealers are always instructed to vary the speed and the number of rotations to prevent any possibility of making the outcome predictable.

Interestingly enough, he said that some dealers do indeed begin the spin of the ball, and let go of the ball at almost precisely the same spots on the wheel-head, and over a period of time will actually wear a groove in the track. To counter this, most casinos will rotate the wheel-head a few inches each week or so, to prevent a groove from forming.

More so, some dealers aware of the system, will purposely let their fingers brush the wheel as they spin the ball, thereby slowing the wheel ever so slightly, but enough to throw off the clocker.

Can A Roulette Dealer Affect The Outcome?

That's a good question! Can certain experienced dealers really influence the drop of the ball?

I have serious doubts that any roulette dealer, or casino boss, could be precise in exerting any possible influence.

But let's look at this as a matter of degree. We can safely assume that no dealer can make the ball drop in a specific compartment without some sort of trickery. That degree of legitimate skill would be virtually impossible, based on, at the very least, the many deflectors that guard the wheel and catch the ball. I didn't just fall off the onion truck and neither did you.

But isn't it possible that at least some control can be gained, such as 5% or even 10% effectiveness in pin-pointing a "section" of the wheel where the ball might drop?

I'm not suggesting that a roulette dealer will cheat the player. Not at all! I'm suggesting that some dealers might be able to predict an outcome based on their many years of acquiring a "feel" for the speed of the ball, and the speed of the wheel.

What significance does this mean to the player you ask? Well, any value to the dealers of their own ability is academic. The dealers can't spin the ball and then bet on their own spin. But the players can! *It's possible that the dealer's consistent routine in spinning the ball and wheel might occur with astonishing regularity, perhaps unbeknownst to the dealer, and the player who's sharp enough to look for it can base his bets on this perfected routine.*

The essence of timing a dealer is to determine if there is any pattern to the spot on the wheel where the ball is released, and the spot where the ball lands.

As you can see, our concern is not predictability on the part of the dealers, but predictability from the player's standpoint, based on the likelihood that the dealer is following a strict routine from which both might be able to predict, but only the player can act!

What we are talking about is an acquired ability, no matter how slight and no matter how useless to the dealer. An ability that the dealer has fashioned through trials and trials and trials. A technique not of his own choosing, but as a function of his daily routine.

If you continually hit golf balls eight hours a day, five days a week, chances are you'll eventually be ready for the tour! It's the same thing here. But of course the roulette dealer can't really "use" his technique for any personal gain, at least not in *today's* casinos. I've always believed that 99.99% of all casinos today run honest games. And I've never had any reason to doubt that belief.

If you're still not convinced that some experienced roulette dealers can develop a predictable routine (not for *their* value, but for *yours*!), put yourself in their position. You've been working the wheel for years and years. After a while, isn't it likely that you would begin to wonder if you could skillfully control the outcome? Isn't it likely that you would eventually decide to "test" your skill during the course of your long work-day? After all, you're being paid to spin the ball, so you might as well have some fun with it.

Eventually, isn't it possible that you might develop an automatic "delivery," no different than the professional golfer's "automatic swing"? A precise, rhythmic style that might lend some predictability to the game?

Surprisingly, a few dealers I talked to confirmed this notion. In fact, one dealer was quite bold in bragging about his "touch."

Remember, I'm not suggesting that any dealer has developed a skill to cheat you. In fact, I was told about a dealer who would occasionally feel sorry for a particular player and would try to help the player win! I'm not sure what it took to qualify for the "help," other than (a) you were losing badly, (b) you reminded him of his mother, or (c) you reminded him of Bo Derek.

I'm not a roulette dealer, so I can't tell you what goes through their minds, and I can't tell you in fact that a skill can be developed. Allowing plenty of room for exaggeration, who's to say that a dealer with a lot of years under his belt can't provide at least a little influence? Who's to say that a dealer has never fell victim to his good Samaritan values? And who's to say what might happen if you walk up to the table with a big, black, smelly cigar?

As you can appreciate, any dealer caught trying to help a player win (or lose), would be fired on the spot, although it would be difficult to prove. This brings to mind the possibility that a skilled roulette dealer could indeed line his own pockets by working in collusion with a player as his partner and splitting the profits.

There are stories about crooked roulette dealers in illegal joints in the old days who could make the ball drop in a narrow section of the wheel where the house had no action or at least the smallest bets. If a big wager was made on 11, the ball would drop on the opposite side of the wheel. *The dealer had the touch.*

But the real point to this discussion should be obvious. If it's indeed possible that certain experienced dealers can affect the outcome by their "skill," doesn't that also suggest that a player could also develop a skill by measuring these same parameters that lead to the same result? Predictability.

Think about it.

Rating Your Options

Here's what we know.

If you're going to try to beat the roulette wheel with a number system or a betting system, with any consistency, forget it. You have no chance!

If you're going to spend lots of time looking for a wheel bias, and if you're lucky enough to find it, the casino will probably change the wheel. That idea certainly has its drawbacks. But it's interesting.

If you're thinking about a hidden computer, complete with all the neat little attachments to clock the wheel, think again. Remember, the device is illegal.

The only possible edge for the player that might work is to consider clocking the dealer. And I have no quarrels with the ethical issue. Otherwise, we wouldn't even be discussing it. There's no device, and obviously no cheating. It's a function of skill and patience . . . and good eyesight.

There's no point in trying to clock a young, or inexperienced dealer. Repetition is the key here. Lots and lots of spins under the belt; years and years of "practice." Sometimes, I'll ask a dealer how long he has been dealing roulette. The longer the better . . . to develop a constant rhythm.

Remember, *the basis of clocking a dealer is to find out if there is any relationship between the spot on the wheel where the ball is released, and the compartment in which the ball falls.*

If you notice that in eight out of ten times, the ball came to rest in a section of the wheel that's directly opposite the release area, that would certainly seem to indicate a possible pattern. Perhaps the ball came to rest near the same release area. That's fine. There's your section to use.

As you can appreciate, the clocker only bets a section of the wheel, making straight-up bets, usually six to eight numbers that are all adjacent on the wheel.

If you're concerned about the highly remote chance that a dealer will try to beat you with his "skill," don't worry about it. Remember, you always place your bet *after* the ball has left his hand!

And that reminds me, try to make your bet as soon as possible. Don't push the limits to the point where the ball is bouncing in the pockets. The dealer might think you're trying to past-post the game!

You must understand that wheel clocking is not an entirely easy affair. There are many snags that you should be aware of. For example, subtle variations in the wheel's speed (or the ball's speed) will make mental wheel clocking totally useless. Although the dealer might be aware of these changes, the player will have great difficulty in detecting them. *The best chance for the player is to clock a dealer who is unaware of your attempts, and unaware for that moment of his natural perfection.*

It's likely that if the dealer knows you're trying to clock him, he'll purposely vary the speed of either the ball or the wheel to beat you at his own game. After all, the dealer has complete control over the parameters that you're trying to measure. Don't let him know that you're making the effort.

If you walk up to a roulette table, stand around for an hour or so with your nose two feet from the wheel, making notes on a scratch pad while jotting down numbers from your hand-held copy of the roulette wheel numbers, my guess is it'll look a little fishy.

The slick wheel clockers, whoever they are, have enough skill and knowledge to actually sit at the table (far left side), watch the ball release, and then mentally determine the relationship to the winning compartment *in degrees*, such as 90° or 270°. After a few spins, if they see any consistency, they'll make a few straight-up bets on the numbers that fall into this same sector, but not by looking at their chart of numbers. That's a give-away. They have the numbers on the wheel *memorized*. And that's not easy!

If you're detected trying to clock the wheel, the floorman will probably keep an eye on you. If you show that you're losing like everyone else, he'll no doubt chuckle a little and walk away. But if you're winning, whether your strategy is working or you're just plain lucky, you'll get some pressure. Either the floorman will instruct the dealer to rush the timeframe in which you can make your wagers, or the dealer will be told to greatly vary the speeds.

At that stage, you might as well sit down, relax, and guess at the numbers like everyone else. Or better yet, try a different game.

I've spent a lot of time on wheel clocking because, quite frankly, it's the only interesting part of the game. The game itself is boring as hell. If that's what it takes to generate a little excitement, why not?

Understand that if you're betting on red/black, odd/even, or low/high numbers, the clocking idea has no value. Obviously, with red and black alternating with each compartment, such bets are strictly a guessing game.

But more importantly, I want you to know that these discussions about wheel clocking have been included in this text simply because it's a part of roulette, and has been for many years. This chapter is about roulette. Without a mention of clocking, the chapter would be incomplete.

These discussions are not to give you false hope, or any wild ideas about owning your own casino! No matter what you might think, there are no guarantees at the roulette table or at any other casino game, regardless of your skills, your memory, or your determination. Like all the games, I suggest you play only for fun, if indeed you decide to play at all. The concept of wheel clocking is something you might want to consider as you make the small table-minimum bets; something that might add to your enjoyment of the game.

At the very least, we can hope that any effort to time the dealer's spin will help to minimize the casino's built-in advantage. But whether your timing efforts work or not, it always pays to shop for a single zero wheel.

CHAPTER 7

Keno

First, I'm going to give you a brief rundown on how the game is played, and then cover each aspect of the game in detail. This way, you won't be overwhelmed by what is basically a simple and easy game.

The keno display board is the most important piece of equipment. A very large version is positioned on the wall, front-center in the casino's main keno lounge. You'll find more, smaller versions of the display board throughout the hotel complex in the many bars and restaurants. All the boards display the exact same information.

The electronic board is simply a configuration of

numbers from 1 to 80, in eight rows of ten numbers each. The numbers are divided into two groups, top and bottom, with numbers from 1 to 40 on top, and from 41 to 80 on the bottom. The separation of these two groups serves no real purpose.

In addition to the display of 80 numbers, the board also indicates a number identifying each individual game. Also, the term "closed" will appear on the board at a certain time signifying that the next game is about to begin and no additional bets will be accepted for that particular game.

How To Play

In preparation for the game, the player must use casino-issued tickets which are readily available near each seat in the keno lounge and at most tables in the restaurants. A supply of black crayons accompanies the tickets and must be used exclusively to mark the tickets—no pens or pencils.

PLAY KENO

PRICE PER WAY	PRICE PER GAME
	1.00

MARK NUMBER OF SPOTS OR WAYS PLAYED

8

NO. OF GAMES	TOTAL PRICE
2	2.00

WINNING TICKETS MUST BE COLLECTED IMMEDIATELY AFTER EACH KENO GAME IS CALLED.

1	2	3	4	5	6	7	8	9	10
11	12	13	14	✗	16	✗	18	19	20
21	22	23	24	25	26	✗	✗	29	30
31	32	33	34	✗	36	37	38	39	40

WE PAY ON MACHINE ISSUED TICKETS   TICKETS WITH ERRORS NOT CORRECTED BEFORE START OF GAME WILL BE ACCEPTED AS ISSUED

41	42	43	44	✗	46	47	48	49	50
51	52	53	54	✗	✗	57	58	59	60
61	62	63	64	65	66	67	68	69	70
71	72	73	74	75	76	77	78	79	80

WE ARE NOT RESPONSIBLE FOR KENO RUNNERS TICKETS NOT VALIDATED BEFORE START OF NEXT GAME.

In marking your ticket, you're guessing which numbers will appear on the display board. The casino selects only 20 numbers out of the possible 80. You are allowed to mark from 1 to 15 numbers by drawing an "X" over the number you wish to pick. If, for example, you mark eight numbers, you'll win if at least five of these numbers are chosen by the casino's machine. If all eight of your numbers appear on the board, you'll win big! **The size of your payoff is determined by the amount you have wagered, the total number of spots (numbers) you have marked, and the total number of spots that you caught (matched).**

Most casinos today use a sophisticated, computerized accounting system that has changed the format of the typical keno ticket. Until recently, the manual systems featured tickets that required the player to identify the conditions of his ticket in the far right margin. With the newer technology, the modern-day ticket features boxes at the top of the ticket, plainly marked, for you to provide all the necessary information . . . in addition to your numbers of course.

So, if you've marked eight spots, simply write the number 8 in the large box to the left. Now, we have to know how much you are going to wager. All casinos have different minimums, so ask to find out. Typically, 70 cent minimums are common in downtown Las Vegas, and in Reno. A minimum of $1 is most common on the Vegas "strip."

Schedule Of Minimum Bets

CASINO	MINIMUM BET REQUIREMENT	MINIMUM BET* TO WIN $50,000
Caesars Tahoe (Lake Tahoe)	$ .70	$1.25
Circus Circus (Las Vegas)	.75	2.50
Eldorado (Reno)	1.00	2.50
Landmark (Las Vegas)	1.00	1.00
• Peppermill (Reno)	1.00	1.25
Sands (Las Vegas)	1.00	2.00
Stardust (Las Vegas)	1.00	2.50

*8-spot ticket. Player catches 8 out of 8.
Data in this chart is subject to change without notice. We assume no responsibility for errors or omissions.

This chart represents a brief survey of casinos aimed at helping you understand the "spread" of minimum bet requirements throughout Nevada. In some cases, the minimum bet required to win $50,000 is based on "special" tickets where the payoffs do not follow the standard Keno pay-schedule.

In addition to the variations in minimum bet requirements to win the big jackpot, you must understand that pay-schedules for *all* jackpots can also vary among casinos. **It pays to shop for the best pay-schedules at the lowest betting minimums.**

Incidentally, you must not assume that a casino with a higher minimum bet requirement to win $50,000 is less attractive than other casinos in terms of overall percentages. As I mentioned, some of the minimum bet amounts posted in our chart reflect special tickets where payoffs for other catches are usually less (or nothing) and make up for the apparent discrepancy.

Nonetheless, **always be sure you're betting the minimum amount to win the big jackpot, if you've marked enough numbers to qualify.** Always check with the casino at the time you play by asking the keno writer "What is the minimum amount I must bet to have a chance to win $50,000?"

In some cases, the minimum amount might actually be less than the amounts shown in the pay-schedules, since few casinos, if any, show the schedules in multiples of $1 or fractions thereof. Always check first!

In addition to the ticket blanks and crayons, the casino also provides a brochure that outlines the payout schedules for all the different betting levels based on the number of spots you've marked. If you've marked 8 spots, your ticket is called an "8-spot." So, look at the brochure under "8-spot" and determine how much you want to bet. You'll see that the payoff progresses in a linear fashion as your betting amount increases.

The following pay-schedule is typical of many casinos. However, the pay-schedules are not all the same. You must be prepared to shop for the best payouts at the best rates. *I've limited the schedule to ten numbers because the percentages against the player tend to increase as the numbers increase.* Besides, the odds of winning the big jackpots on the higher number tickets are prohibitive. In fact, it's nearly impossible!

Most experienced keno players limit their tickets to no more than eight spots. The most popular are four, six, and eight-number tickets.

Note that the pay-schedule is directly based on the amount you have wagered. For example, on an 8-spot ticket, the payoff for catching five numbers is $13.50 for a $1.50 bet; $27 for a $3 bet; $54 for a $6 bet and so on. As your bet doubles, so does the payoff. Since this pay-schedule is provided by the Desert Inn, and the Desert Inn offers a $1 minimum bet, a $1 bet would pay $9 if you catch the same five spots. $1 is one-third of $3, and $9 is one-third of $27.

Once you've determined how much you wish to wager, enter this amount in the box at the top-right of the ticket marked "price per game." When you write in the amount, do not use dollar-signs or decimals. If cents are involved, underline the cents amount to distinguish it from the dollar value. Don't ask me why this is important, but that's the way the casino wants it done.

If you are going to play two games with that ticket for $1 each, the "price per game" is $1 and the "total price" is $2. Usually, you can play up to five consecutive games with the same ticket.

A frequent rule with the new type of accounting system is that you must wait until all the games you've marked have been played before you can collect any winnings, regardless of which game hit. But check it out to be sure. You only have until the start of the next game to collect your winnings. Most casinos state clearly on their tickets

MARK 1 NUMBER

Winning Spots	$3.00 Ticket Pays	$6.00 Ticket Pays	$9.00 Ticket Pays	$1.50 Ticket Pays
1	9.00	18.00	27.00	4.50

MARK 2 NUMBERS

Winning Spots	$3.00 Ticket Pays	$6.00 Ticket Pays	$9.00 Ticket Pays	$1.50 Ticket Pays
2	36.00	72.00	108.00	18.00

MARK 3 NUMBERS

Winning Spots	$3.00 Ticket Pays	$6.00 Ticket Pays	$9.00 Ticket Pays	$1.50 Ticket Pays
2	3.00	6.00	9.00	1.50
3	126.00	252.00	378.00	63.00

MARK 4 NUMBERS

Winning Spots	$3.00 Ticket Pays	$6.00 Ticket Pays	$9.00 Ticket Pays	$1.50 Ticket Pays
2	3.00	6.00	9.00	1.50
3	12.00	24.00	36.00	6.00
4	336.00	672.00	1,008.00	168.00

MARK 5 NUMBERS

Winning Spots	$3.00 Ticket Pays	$6.00 Ticket Pays	$9.00 Ticket Pays	$1.50 Ticket Pays
3	6.00	12.00	18.00	3.00
4	60.00	120.00	180.00	30.00
5	1,440.00	2,880.00	4,320.00	720.00

MARK 6 NUMBERS

Winning Spots	$3.00 Ticket Pays	$6.00 Ticket Pays	$9.00 Ticket Pays	$1.50 Ticket Pays
3	3.00	6.00	9.00	1.50
4	12.00	24.00	36.00	6.00
5	264.00	528.00	792.00	132.00
6	4,440.00	8,880.00	13,320.00	2,220.00

MARK 7 NUMBERS

Winning Spots	$3.00 Ticket Pays	$6.00 Ticket Pays	$9.00 Ticket Pays	$1.50 Ticket Pays
4	6.00	12.00	18.00	3.00
5	72.00	144.00	216.00	36.00
6	1,080.00	2,160.00	3,240.00	540.00
7	15,000.00	30,000.00	45,000.00	7,500.00

MARK 8 NUMBERS

Winning Spots	$3.00 Ticket Pays	$6.00 Ticket Pays	$9.00 Ticket Pays	$1.50 Ticket Pays
5	27.00	54.00	81.00	13.50
6	255.00	510.00	765.00	127.50
7	4,500.00	9,000.00	13,500.00	2,250.00
8	50,000.00	50,000.00	50,000.00	25,000.00

MARK 9 NUMBERS

Winning Spots	$3.00 Ticket Pays	$6.00 Ticket Pays	$9.00 Ticket Pays	$1.50 Ticket Pays
5	9.00	18.00	27.00	4.50
6	120.00	240.00	360.00	60.00
7	900.00	1,800.00	2,700.00	450.00
8	12,000.00	24,000.00	36,000.00	6,000.00
9	50,000.00	50,000.00	50,000.00	30,000.00

MARK 10 NUMBERS

Winning Spots	$3.00 Ticket Pays	$6.00 Ticket Pays	$9.00 Ticket Pays	$1.50 Ticket Pays
5	6.00	12.00	18.00	3.00
6	54.00	108.00	162.00	27.00
7	390.00	780.00	1,170.00	195.00
8	2,880.00	5,760.00	8,640.00	1,440.00
9	11,400.00	22,800.00	34,200.00	5,700.00
10	50,000.00	50,000.00	50,000.00	37,500.00

Courtesy: Desert Inn

that *"Winning tickets must be collected immediately after each keno game is called."* You only have a few minutes. If you miss the deadline, your winnings are forfeited.

If you're playing in the casino's restaurant instead of the keno lounge, don't rely on the keno runner who has serviced your ticket to meet this deadline. Again, most casinos run a standard disclaimer on the ticket blanks. *"We are not responsible for keno runners tickets not validated before start of next game."*

If your payoff is a big one, you're allowed to knock over your chair, the busboy, and anyone else in your way to get to the main keno counter in time. Run!

All casinos have their own horror stories about unfortunate players who ended up in the maze of gift shops looking for the keno counter, as the next game started. By that time, their winning ticket was only a worthless piece of paper. If you're playing in the casino's restaurant, make sure you know where the main keno counter is located. That's good advice especially in the larger casinos.

Experienced keno players always prefer to present their own ticket (both for acceptance and validation) and to do this, they must be situated in or near the main keno area.

Upon submitting your ticket and the amount of your wager to the writer, the numbers you picked (and the conditions) will be fed into the computerized accounting system that automatically spits out a similar ticket for you to use as a reference during the next game. The computer-issued ticket will have the same numbers marked, and will list the numbers numerically, and in chronological order. In addition, all the conditions you specified—number of games, amount of wager, etc., will be plainly shown on the ticket's record. The machine-issued ticket is, however, more than a receipt for your wager. In most cases, that ticket is what the casino will pay against, not your original ticket. If there's an error in transferring your original ticket to the machine-issued ticket, the player must notify the writer immediately. Otherwise, it's likely that the machine-issued ticket, with the error, will become the ticket of record. But to be sure, always ask the ticket writers before you play. This rule, like so many others, differs among casinos. Most keno tickets carry a disclaimer similar to: *"We pay on machine issued tickets—tickets with errors not corrected before start of game will be accepted as issued."*

With your machine-issued ticket in hand, you're now ready to sit back and relax, and wait for the numbers to appear on the giant keno board.

Since this section deals with the presentation of your original ticket to the keno writers, it's the right spot to mention the "old" way of doing this before the advent of the computer-accounting systems. The "old" game was called a "brush" game, and the keno writer simply took your original ticket and made a hand-written copy with a brush using India Ink. The original ticket was inserted into a machine that would stamp the date, time, game number and counter position, to insure the integrity of the ticket. Your original ticket would be kept at the counter, and if a winning ticket was presented, that original ticket (not the brushed copy) would be retrieved and checked for the win. In other words, with the old brush game, the casino paid on the "original" ticket.

Since there are still many casinos who still use the brush, make sure that you are aware which type of game you're playing, and more importantly, on which ticket—your original or the copy, will the casino pay.

Example of a ticket to be used with the "brush" game, before the advent of the computer accounting system. Note that the number of spots marked is to be written in the right margin. The price of the ticket is entered in the box at the top right.

Incidentally, the casino limits its liability for each game to $50 thousand. Virtually all keno tickets carry the disclaimer: *"$50,000 limit to aggregate players each game."*

This simply means that if the total amount of winnings among all the players for a particular game exceeds $50 thousand, each player will receive a pro-rated share of the $50 thousand, based on the relative size of the player's win and the amount of all the others that won also.

Here we are talking about winning $50 thousand like it happens every day. Since the casinos raised the keno limits from $25 thousand to $50 thousand in 1979, there are some casinos who have never had a $50 thousand winner! Certain players might have hit the right number of spots, but didn't have enough wagered to win the big prize. Big keno jackpots are few and far between.

Selecting The Numbers

Now that we understand the basics of the game, let's find out how the casino actually selects the numbers that will determine if your ticket wins or loses.

Today, casinos use either of two popular systems of randomly selecting numbers. Both systems use ping-pong balls, each with a number from 1 to 80 printed on the ball. Perhaps the most popular system features a rotating "squirrel" cage (without the squirrel) in which all the balls are thoroughly mixed. Another system incorporates an air-blower concept that disperses the balls by blowing an air current into a large glass bowl.

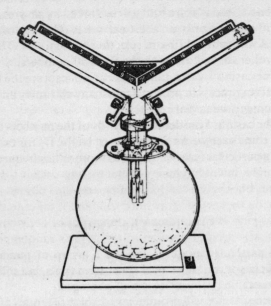

BLOWER SYSTEM CAPTIVE BALL DEVICE
Courtesy: Tripp Plastics, Reno, NV.

In greater analysis, the wire cage system tumbles the balls in such a manner that it is very doubtfull any ball could be biased in its selection. The opening at the bottom will accept one ball at a time upon command of the operator; a gentle spring forces the ball into the display tube. With the blower system, all the balls are bouncing into the air with complete randomness, not by a moving container, but by the forces of air pressure. To activate the ball selection process, the operator triggers a mechanism that opens a long tube through the center of the bowl, into which a ball will be forced by air pressure to fill one of the two rabbit-ear tubes. One ear of the tubes will be filled first in selecting 10 numbers. Then, the other ear will fill with the final 10 numbers.

The casino's video-tape cameras will capture the ball selection process to protect against any chicanery and to document the actual results.

The casinos keep detailed records of the numbers that come up, over weeks and weeks of trials. If, for example, a particular number appeared more or less frequently than the law of averages dictated, the casino would simply change the ball! Of course, the law of averages is really the law of large numbers, and it takes tens of thousands, even hundreds of thousands of decisions to form any decided opinion of the game's randomness. **One particular number, or even a group of numbers might lag or run ahead over short-term trials, but still be accountable to the strict law of averages.**

Some casinos will prominently display the totals of all numbers that have been chosen over the prior week, and most all casinos will give a player a listing of the numbers as recorded by a computer. The casinos are convinced there is no bias in their system. They encourage the player to chart the prior results. As you can appreciate, the casino won't encourage you to do anything that might help you beat them. But if it adds to your enjoyment of the game, by all means keep records. Just remember that *any deviation in probability over a few hundred games is perfectly normal, and adds nothing to the game's predictability.*

The Straight Ticket

In our example, I've shown a typical 6-spot straight ticket. With this type of ticket, the player will only win if at least three numbers are caught. Technically, the player will win only if at least four spots are caught because at keno, all payoffs are "for" your bet, not

PLAY KENO

MARK NUMBER OF SPOTS OR WAYS PLAYED		

PRICE PER WAY	PRICE PER GAME
	3°°

6

NO. OF GAMES	TOTAL PRICE
1	3°°

WINNING TICKETS MUST BE COLLECTED IMMEDIATELY AFTER EACH KENO GAME IS CALLED

1	2	3	X	X	6	7	8	9	10
11	12	13	14	15	X	X	18	19	20
21	22	23	24	25	26	27	28	29	30
31	32	33	34	X	36	37	38	39	40

WE PAY ON MACHINE ISSUED TICKETS   TICKETS WITH ERRORS NOT CORRECTED BEFORE START OF GAME WILL BE ACCEPTED AS ISSUED

41	42	43	44	45	X	47	48	49	50
51	52	53	54	55	56	57	58	59	60
61	62	63	64	65	66	67	68	69	70
71	72	73	74	75	76	77	78	79	80

WE ARE NOT RESPONSIBLE FOR KENO RUNNERS TICKETS NOT VALIDATED BEFORE START OF NEXT GAME "to" as in other casino games. In other words, *the casino does not return your original wager.* So, in the case of a 6-spot ticket, catching three spots means you break even. You haven't won a penny. "Winning" $3 is not winning at all if you bet $3 and the casino keeps your bet. Similarly, if you caught four spots for a payoff of $12, you won $9, not $12, assuming your bet was $3.

PLAY KENO

MARK NUMBER OF SPOTS OR WAYS PLAYED

2/6

PRICE PER WAY	PRICE PER GAME
3°°	6°°
NO. OF GAMES	TOTAL PRICE
1	6°°

WINNING TICKETS MUST BE COLLECTED IMMEDIATELY AFTER EACH KENO GAME IS CALLED

1	2	3	X	X	X	7	8	9	10
11	12	13	X	X	X	17	18	19	20
21	22	23	24	25	26	27	28	29	30
31	32	33	34	35	36	37	38	39	40

WE PAY ON MACHINE ISSUED TICKETS   TICKETS WITH ERRORS NOT CORRECTED BEFORE START OF GAME WILL BE ACCEPTED AS ISSUED

41	42	43	44	45	46	47	48	49	50
51	52	53	54	55	56	X	X	X	60
61	62	63	64	65	66	X	X	X	70
71	72	73	74	75	76	77	78	79	80

WE ARE NOT RESPONSIBLE FOR KENO RUNNERS TICKETS NOT VALIDATED BEFORE START OF NEXT GAME.

The Split Ticket

In our illustration, we've marked two sets of six numbers. Each set in casino parlance is called a "way." Our split ticket is really two ways of hitting six numbers — two 6-spot tickets on one ticket.

The ticket could have easily been written with the top grouping of numbers on one ticket, and the bottom grouping of numbers on another ticket. It's obviously easier to mark on one ticket, and that's what the split ticket is for.

Notice that the total amount of our wager is $6 because we're playing two ways at $3 each.

Whenever a fraction-like number appears in the large box, the top number represents the number of ways, and the bottom number represents the number of spots. The number is not a fraction; merely two numbers separated by a line.

The Way Ticket

A way ticket is nothing more than groupings of numbers added together to form different "ways" in which to win.

In this other example of a way ticket, I've marked twelve numbers in groups of three. Note that there are four groups circled. There are six ways to form a 6-spot ticket using any two groups of the four. But how do I know that there are six ways? It's a question that surprisingly few authors answer in the many keno books that are available.

The answer comes from our high school algebra text, the section that dealt with finding the number of combinations of N things taken R at a time. Remember it? Remember algebra? Remember high school?

The simple formula is:

$$C = \frac{(\text{total number of circles})!}{(\text{number of circles needed})!}$$

Incidentally, (!) means "factorial," and for any given number, it's the product of that number times consecutive whole numbers down to 1. For example, the factorial of 4 is 4 x 3 x 2 x 1, or 24.

In this equation, the total number of numerals on top (the numerator) must equal the number of numerals on the bottom (the denominator). And, we must begin our factorial with the numeral 1 on the bottom. *Always do the bottom number first, since that will determine how many numerals we'll use on top.* Got it?

$$C = \frac{4 \times 3}{1 \times 2} = \frac{12}{2} = 6$$

To further explain how we arrived at our answer, we know we needed two groups because we want a 6-spot ticket, and each group contains three numbers. So the bottom number in our equation will be 1 x 2. If we need three groups, the bottom number would have been 1 x 2 x 3. Since we placed two numerals in our bottom number, we can only use two numerals on top. And, the top number is going to be 4(!) which is 4 x 3 x 2 x 1. But we only use the first two of these digits, because only two digits are on the bottom. It bears repeating. *We must have the same number of numerals on the top and bottom of our equation in order for it to work.*

If we wanted to know how many ways we can form a 6-spot ticket, using six groups of two numbers, here's how it would look:

$$\frac{6 \times 5 \times 4}{1 \times 2 \times 3} = 20$$

To quickly solve the fraction, try to factor it so that the numeral 1 is left as the denominator. In our example, the quantity (2 x 3) in the denominator is obviously 6 which will "cancel" the 6 in the numerator. All we have left is 5 x 4.

There are 20 ways to make a 6-spot ticket using six groups of two numbers.

It should be pointed out that increasing the number of ways on your ticket only increases your chances of winning by having more combinations of the same numbers working for you. *It does not change the percentages against you.* And, of course, it increases the total cost of your ticket.

Here's a chart that lists the most popular combinations of numbers and groups to form way tickets.

4-SPOT WAY TICKETS

NUMBER OF GROUPS	NUMBERS IN EACH GROUP	NUMBER OF WAYS
3	2	3
4	2	6
5	2	10

6-SPOT WAY TICKETS

NUMBER OF GROUPS	NUMBERS IN EACH GROUP	NUMBER OF WAYS
4	2	4
5	2	10
3	3	3
4	3	6
5	3	10
6	3	15

8-SPOT WAY TICKETS

NUMBER OF GROUPS	NUMBERS IN EACH GROUP	NUMBER OF WAYS
3	4	3
4	4	6
5	4	10
6	4	15

In many casinos, the player is allowed to bet a way ticket at less than the minimum posted on the casino's pay schedules. If the minimum bet advertised is $1, it's possible that you can wager as little as 50 cents on way tickets. If the minimum is 70 cents, each way could be only 35 cents, making the way ticket not as expensive as you might have thought. Remember, the minimums vary

from one casino to another. And, cutting your bet in half
will also reduce any winnings by one-half.

The Combination Ticket

Now that we have the easy charts to go by, marking
a combination ticket is easy. The combination ticket is
a fancy way-ticket for more than one total of spots.

Again, our illustration will better explain it.

I've marked ten numbers in groups of two. All ten numbers give us a 1-way 10-spot. Using any two groups, there are ten ways of making a 4-spot. And, using any three groups together there are ten ways of making a 6-spot.

Now, assuming we can bet 50 cents per way, our total cost per game will be $10.50 (21 times 50¢). We have 21 different ways to win.

On our sample ticket, I've pretended to play this ticket for two consecutive games so our total cost wil be $21.00. This is purely for illustrative purposes. At no time would I recommend that you wager $21 over the course of two games. Keep your bets at a safe and sensible level. The casino has a big edge on every ticket!

The King Ticket

Here we have a ticket where one circled number (the king) combines with other numbers or groups to produce more ways. In our example, number 19 is our king, and combined with the two circled groups will form two 5-spots. All the numbers together make a 9-spot ticket.

If the two groups of numbers were not circled, we would have a 1-way 8-spot and 1-way 9-spot ticket, ignoring the king in one case, and using it in the other.

The Percentages

I'm not going to kid you. The percentages are steep against the player. More so than any other game. But let's find out why.

Most players would assume that the house advantage at keno is high because the jackpots are so high. But that's not the reason. Don't confuse the house percentage with the odds of winning.

The high odds of winning are what make the jackpots big. That's the only way the casino can afford to offer such large payoffs. It has nothing to do with the percentages.

The reasons that the casino has such a big edge are largely two-fold. First, the cost of running the game is quite high. Keno is one of the most labor intense games in the casino. Suffice to say, the casino has a huge overhead.

The other reason for the high percentages against the player is the average "handle" of the game. The handle refers to the amount of action from all the players. On a typical weekend day, a strip casino might run 200 games. For the 200 games, perhaps 6,000 to 8,000 tickets might have been played. The average cost of the ticket is about $2. Obviously, there are a lot of tickets played for $1 or less to compensate for the few tickets that run $5 and higher. From the casino's viewpoint, keno is considered a "cheap" game. The handle for the day might reach $15 thousand. And we all know that "action" of that size could take place at the baccarat tables in a matter of minutes! Not days. High rollers don't play keno!

Baccarat, craps, and blackjack produce a much larger handle for the casino. They have so much money "at risk" from the players that a smaller percentage of profit (the casino calls it "hold") is perfectly acceptable to them. Which would you rather have, 5% of $200 thousand, or 25% of $10 thousand? Yes, 5% is about the average hold at blackjack and craps. And 25% is indeed the number at keno. And it can even go higher. Over 40%! But, to make up for the high costs of operating the game, and the fact that the wagers are relatively small, the percentage has to be that high, otherwise the casino couldn't afford to offer the game.

There's yet another reason for the high percentages. Plainly, it's the casino's greed. From time to time, the casino has experimented with reduced percentages but the result had no bearing on the handle. In other words, players didn't respond. The handle didn't increase, so why offer the better game. If the same players are willing to play at 25%, instead of 15% for example, why bother with it. The casino will take as much as they can. Business is business.

The easiest way to prove the 25% casino advantage is to look at a 1-spot ticket. We know the casino selects 20 numbers out of 80, so the odds of picking one number are 3 to 1. The 3 to 1 odds can be simply expressed as 60 numbers that are not selected to 20 numbers that are. 60 to 20 is obviously 3 to 1. Now, if the correct odds are indeed 3 to 1, to make it a fair game (no house advantage), the casino should pay you 3 to 1. But they don't. The payout schedule for a 1-spot ticket appears as if they do; according to most schedules the casino will pay $3 for your one winning spot. But don't forget, the casino keeps your wager. At other games, blackjack for example, if you win, you receive your winnings *and* your original bet. But not at keno. The casino keeps it! In effect, that makes the payoff 2 to 1, not 3 to 1. The difference is one losing unit out of four, or 25%. If you played a 1-spot four times, you should lose your $1 bet three times and "win" $2 once. You've invested $4 over four plays, and end up with $3. Like I said, losing $1 over four plays is a 25% game against you.

All the payoffs have been carefully devised so that the casino holds at least 25% *over the course of all payout possibilities, including the big jackpots.*

Incidentally, the odds of picking eight out of eight numbers are 230,114 to 1! For a $3 bet (a minimum to earn the giant jackpot in some casinos), the payoff is $50 thousand. If there were no other payoffs for smaller catches, the payoff for catching all eight numbers should be over $690 thousand to make it a fair game. When all four payoff possibilities of an 8-spot ticket are taken into account (5,6,7, and 8 catches), the casino advantage is nearly 30%.

And speaking of odds, most keno players really don't want to know what the odds are beyond the common 8-spot ticket. But I'm going to tell you anyhow. Catching ten out of ten numbers is nearly 9 million to 1! And twelve out of twelve numbers is almost 500 million to 1! Catching fifteen out of fifteen numbers is way out beyond the solar system! To my knowledge, no player has ever done it. Stick with the 4-spot, 6-spot, and 8-spot tickets where you at least have a "down-to-earth" chance of winning.

The bottom line on all this should be obvious. Don't play keno for serious money! Have fun with it; enjoy yourself; but don't get any wild ideas. The only serious money attached to this game is in the casino's counting-room!

CHAPTER 8

The Sports Book

It should be made clear that the thrust of this chapter is to the legal side of sports betting in Nevada where the industry has reached unprecedented levels of sophistication, technology, and acceptance. The great majority of sports books today have climbed out of their "chalk on the wall" image and offer the player an attractive, comfortable, and sometimes lavish ambience...complete with crystal chandeliers, velvet wallpapering, and cushy carpeting. All a player has to do to get this message is walk through the sports book at Caesars Palace or the Las Vegas Hilton where there are multiscreen projection systems for satellite feeds of three to four games at a time, a 90-foot long computerized display-board for all the betting information, row upon row of plush theater-type seating, adjoining restaurants and bars, and the most sophisticated computer system for recording and monitoring all betting activity. Suffice to say, it's a long way from what it was like twenty years ago.

The idea of betting on sporting events is frowned upon by the team organizations themselves, especially from league headquarters. And it's frowned upon by most churches, except on bingo night. But the encouragement to indeed bet a game or two comes from many unexpected sources. For example, it's virtually impossible to watch a game on television, especially football, where the announcer or pre-game analyst does not mention a betting line. In fact, many so-called experts will brazenly make their selections *against the spread,* just prior to game-time.

During football season, cable TV airs several programs featuring former pro players or sports service personalities rating the weekend games *against the spread,* not unlike critics rating a movie.

Even the newspapers get into the act by publishing the point-spreads for football and basketball and the money-lines for baseball. Many large newspapers include weekly columns featuring their own sportswriters picking the winners *against the spread.*

For some people, a bet on a game just makes it more "interesting," and that's all. For others, it simply gives them a chance to participate in a contest instead of being a neutral spectator. But for most players in Nevada, sports betting is a contest all by itself. It's the player vs.

the sports book, no different than the player vs. the casino.

After a game has been played that you watched, consider your response to someone who asks, "How did your team do?" If you like the winning team, your answer is "They won." If it's your favorite team or alma mater, your answer is "We won." If you had a bet on the team, your answer is "*I* won."

The Point Spread

During football or basketball season, most all sports books offer a "point-spread" to handicap the differences among teams. If, for example, Cleveland is playing Pittsburgh in a football game and you know that Cleveland is a much better team, you can expect to find out that Cleveland is indeed the favorite and will be "giving" a certain number of points to the underdog Steelers. It's no different than when you're playing golf with a friend who is much better than you are. To make the contest a fair opportunity for both, the better player must spot the other a few strokes, depending on exactly how much better your friend really is.

So, getting back to our football game, **if Cleveland is considered to be a touchdown better than Pittsburgh, then Cleveland can be said to be favored by 7 points. The point-spread is 7. And on the board, the number " – 7" will be written beside Cleveland's team name,** which is the Browns. Some sports books use only the team names, not the cities, when listing games.

If you bet this game and decide to take Cleveland, you

must win by more than 7 points to collect on your bet. If Pittsburgh wins the game outright, or loses by 6 points or less, you've lost your bet. If the game ends up 21-14 Cleveland, there is no decision on the wager and it is returned to you.

It can also be said that Cleveland is "minus 7," or that Pittsburgh is "plus 7." One or the other, *but not both,* otherwise the point-spread would be 14 points. If the game ends up 14 to 10 with Cleveland winning, you lost your bet if you took Cleveland because with the point-spread taken into account, Pittsburgh "covered the spread." Subtracting 7 points from Cleveland's score gives Pittsburgh the edge 10 to 7. But don't think of the spread in exactly that way. More correctly, think that Cleveland *only won by 4,* and that wasn't enough to cover the spread of 7 points. Don't convert the spread into a different final score than it really was. The score was 14 to 10, and Cleveland didn't cover. That's the way to think it through. If Cleveland had scored *18* points to Pittsburgh's 10, then Cleveland would have indeed covered the spread and you would have won your bet, taking Cleveland −7.

Fortunately, this same rule of the point-spread also applies to basketball games. But unfortunately, it doesn't apply to baseball, as we'll learn later.

Football "Juice"

Like a casino operation, the sports book itself does not actually gamble, or at least would prefer not to. A casino offers gambling, but the gambling is done on the part of the players, not by the casino. Since all games have a particular house advantage, the more players play, the more the casino wins. Over a long term, the casino never loses.

The sports book operation is set up along these same lines, and with rare exception, never loses over the long term either. It's a function of the quantity of bettors, the accuracy of the lines, and of course, good management.

In order to establish a "house edge," the sports book requires that all wagers on football and basketball (all games based on a point-spread) are made at 11 to 10 odds. This means that all bets, whether for the favorite or the underdog, must be made "against the odds," in addition to against the point-spread. For example, if you want to bet $100, a winning selection will earn you $90.90 based on 11 to 10 odds. If you want to *win* $100, you must risk $110. To avoid the confusing payoffs, always make your bets in consideration of the 11 to 10 odds, such as $55 to win $50, $11 to win $10, or $220 to win $200. Regardless of the size of your bet, always remember that you're betting against the odds, and against the point-spread.

To understand how the sports book makes money, let's reduce the sports book's action, in theory, to two players, each taking one side and laying $110. Now, the sports book is holding $220 (called the "handle"). Assuming the final score is not the exact point-spread, and that the betting line did not move, the sports book will pay one winner $100 and return the $110 wager. What the sports book has left is its profit of $10. **As a percentage, its profit is 4½% (10 ÷ 220).**

It's obvious that if the opening line correctly split the bettor's opinion, and the sports book indeed received equal 2-way action, it earns the juice *no matter which team wins.*

Many new bettors, aware that they have to bet 10% more than they can win, incorrectly assume that the percentage against them is 10%. As you can see, the actual percentage must be based over the course of both probabilities: win or lose. Experienced players who know this still believe that the true percentage is 5%, but of course that number is wrong also, as we've just proven. We can assume their error is using $200 as the handle instead of the actual $220.

Since many new bettors are surprised that the juice is "only" 4½%, let's prove it again a different way, the same way that most casino-game percentages are determined. At the roulette table for example, if the correct odds are 37 to 1 for hitting any one number, yet the casino will only pay 35 to 1, we simply divide the number of units the casino has "shorted" us (2) by the total of both numbers in the correct odds expression (38). Two divided by 38 is 5.26%, which is the percentage against the player at roulette. Similarly, when betting football, we are "shorted" 1/11 of a unit. Divided by the total of both numbers in the correct odds expression (the correct odds are obviously 1 to 1) we yield the same 4½%.

$$\frac{\frac{1}{11}}{2} = \frac{1}{11} \cdot \frac{1}{2} = \frac{1}{22} = .045$$

Line Movements

Earlier, we mentioned that the sports book will earn its 4½ % juice only if the betting line has not moved, and if an equal number of dollars are bet on both sides. If either criterion is not met (it rarely is), the sports book might win more, win less, or actually lose. In other words, the sports book is gambling. Of course, we would also have to assume that the final score did not rest exactly on the point-spread. Now, let's analyze each aspect of all this to see how any variations can affect the sports book's profits, and perhaps the bettor's profits too.

If the opening line is not on target, the sports book will not get equal 2-way betting action, which of course is what it wants. If indeed the opening line was not perfectly suited for 2-way equal action, the sports book's option is to adjust the line. If too much money is coming in on the favorite, it might make the spread a half-point or even one full point higher to discourage more betting on the favorite and increase the action on the underdog. Once the betting action begins to right itself, the sports book might again adjust the line by moving it back down, but only if the action warrants. Since some sports books accept wagers of $10,000 (or more) on regular season football games, you can see that only a few bets, if all one-sided, can quickly make the line move. It's not unusual for a football line to move two points when the action gets heavy. In that case, a large line movement is not necessarily because the line was wrong at the outset, but could be caused by unusually heavy one-sided betting by only two or three players.

Accordingly, the player might find different lines by shopping the many sports books available. Indeed, shopping for the best line is critical to a successful bettor. As we mentioned, differences of 2 points or more are not that unusual. The line movement might help the sports book by balancing the money on both sides, but it also might help certain bettors by giving them less points to lay on a favorite, or more points to take on the underdog, depending on which direction the line actually moves.

Although the sports book moves a betting line in its own best interests, sometimes it backfires, and ends up costing the sports book huge sums of cash. Here's how it can happen. Let's say Dallas opens at −6 against Detroit. Early betting is brisk and most of it is on Dallas. To counter this one-sided action, the sports book decides to move the line all the way to −8. If a bettor took Dallas at −6 before the line moved, and then took the underdog Lions at +8, what do you suppose would happen if the game ended up 28-21 Dallas? What happens is the bettor wins both bets! The bookie got "middled," as the term is called, but a more appropriate term for it is "killed!" That's the risk the sports book takes when line movements are significant.

Incidentally, the sports book is also vulnerable to losing one side and "pushing" on the other (pushing means a tie). That would be the case in our example if the final score was either a 6-point or 8-point win for Dallas. In this instance, the sports book is said to have been "sided."

If the betting line did not move, and the point-spread did not include a half-point, it's possible that the entire contest is a push. If the point-spread is 10, and the final score has the favorite winning by 10, the sports book has to return *all* the bets. No action, no profit.

A ½-point in the betting line insures that the game will not fall exactly on the spread. At this number, all bets will be either won or lost . . . no ties.

If indeed you lost the game by a half-point, you might as well have lost it by 20! A loss is a loss. And don't make excuses for your lousy luck by blaming it on some poor player who threw up an air-ball in the closing seconds, or who couldn't make just one of two free-throws to save it for you. *You'll win some games that you should have lost, and you'll lose some games that you should have won.* Accept your losses as easily as you accept your wins.

Sometimes two teams will be evenly matched. When this happens, the term "Pick," "Pick 'Em," or simply "PK" will be shown on the board in place of a point-spread number.

In the case of a pick 'em game, you will lay 11 to 10, as usual, on either team to win outright . . . no points either way. A tie game in this case is a push; your bet will be refunded.

But remember, the oddsmaker doesn't necessarily believe the teams are evenly matched in a pick 'em game, but that *the betting public believes* the teams are evenly matched. That's a big difference sometimes. What's really important in pick 'em contests, or any games with a point-spread for that matter, is whether or not you believe the line truly reflects the scoring potential of two opposing teams. If it doesn't, in your humble opinion, then you've found a game worth considering.

It should be pointed out that betting lines are not as stable as they were in the past. Line movements can be quite severe on Mondays when the lines are first posted during football season, and the avid bettor must be quick to find any mistake. Within hours, the sports book will know exactly how successful the line is, and *within minutes* will make any needed changes. Most often, the line will become rock-solid by midday, and continue through the week—numbers that remarkably, week after week, split the betting public right down the middle.

The Money-Line

Baseball betting is based on a "money-line," which is really a means of rating two opposing teams in terms of "odds." Unlike football or basketball where teams are handicapped by a differential in scoring potential as we've just learned, baseball is handicapped on the basis of a team's likelihood of winning, not by how many runs, but just winning.

To make this point absolutely clear, think of football or basketball as being rated in terms of points—how many points is one team better than the other. But in baseball, think of the game as being measured solely by one team's chances of winning, regardless of the final score.

To do this effectively, odds are quoted on the favorite team, such as 7 to 5 odds. And here's just one area where the picture gets a little cloudy. Usually whenever odds are quoted, the first number in the odds expression is the number of times a win will *not* happen. The second number is the number of times it will. The total of both numbers in the odds expression is the total number of theoretical contests it will take to develop a true relationship between winning and losing.

As an example, the odds are 37 to 1 at the roulette table of hitting any one number on the next spin. Since there are 38 compartments on the wheel where the ball might land, you can easily see why the odds are 37 to 1. At the race track, if a horse goes off at 20 to 1, it will be lucky to get out of the starting gate. The bettor has only a one in 21 chance of winning. These examples support the method of quoting odds in virtually all gambling events, the odds *of* winning. But in baseball, sometimes the odds are quoted *against* winning, and the first number in the odds expression may or may not represent the winning events.

So, in the case of our example earlier, where a team is favored by 7 to 5 odds, it means that the favorite should win 7 out of 12 times. The oddsmakers have determined that 12 games are enough to accurately rate the two teams. Seven times the favorite will probably win, and 5 times will probably lose. Of course, we don't know which games will be winners or losers, or for that matter, if the odds will turn out anywhere near what the oddsmakers have predicted, but we can conclude that the favorite has a 58% chance of winning *in each game* of our theoretical set. Yes, some bettors prefer to reduce odds to percentages. In our example, 7/12 is 58% (7 ÷ 12).

Now, let's put names on our two teams and see if we can make any sense out of all this. Let's say the Mets are the favored team, and Boston is the underdog. It's the World Series, and the odds are being quoted on the opening game. The Mets are 7 to 5 favorites over the Sox.

The oddsmakers have also installed the Mets as an 11 to 5 favorite against winning the entire Series. OK, that's easy enough, the Mets have a better than 2 to 1 chance of winning; so they say. If the Series were 16 games instead of the best of 7, the oddsmakers believe the Mets would win 11 times.

But at the beginning of the season, many months prior, these same oddsmakers made the Mets 8 to 1 hopefuls of winning the Series. Does this mean the Mets have an 8 out of 9 chance of winning? Of course not. The oddsmakers were quoting the odds *of* winning, not *against* winning. As a percentage, it's only 11%!

Later in the season, just before the league playoffs, newspapers were correctly quoting the Mets as 5 to 8 favorites of winning the Series. After all, the Mets had the best record in baseball and looked invincible. Although the numbers look "turned around," the expression is correct and follows the same form as the 8 to 1 odds quoted at the beginning of the season. The difference is because the Mets *turned it around* and became the odds-on favorite to win it all.

Seven to 5, 8 to 1, 5 to 8, odds of winning, odds against . . . no wonder the average bettor is confused. If the oddsmakers followed the same odds formula throughout the season, then the Mets would be 5 to 7 favorites over Boston in our opening Series game. But it's quoted as 7 to 5 as if we're asking, "What are the odds that the Mets *won't* win it?" Are you still with me?

Converting the odds to a money-line is no cinch either. Here's the way most beginners do it. **Let's consider our 7 to 5 odds as being $70 to $50. Now, let's double the numbers to $140 to $100, same relationship, same odds. Sports books put up the betting numbers on a basis of $100, or just "100." If the Mets are indeed a 7 to 5 favorite, up goes the number "140" beside their name on the board. A minus sign is in front of the number to indicate that they are the favorite.**

Now, if we're going to bet the Mets, assuming you still want to, **we must give the sports book $140 to win $100, or any other amount to be paid in that same ratio. We can wager $70 to win $50, or even $7 to win $5,** although that paltry amount might be under the minimum they accept. Seven dollars just doesn't turn anyone on anymore, especially in Las Vegas.

The best way to convert the "−140" on the board is the same way the sports books themselves do it. Think of it as $1.40 and figure that you can win $1 on every $1.40 you risk. Give the sports book $14; if the Mets win, you win $10 (plus your original $14 is given back of course).

If you like the underdog Sox, you would ideally like to bet $1 to win $1.40 and that would make it a fair proposition. Of course, the sports book wouldn't earn any profit over the long term doing it that way, so he adjusts the actual numbers so that he can make an "honest" living. He'll ask you to risk a little more on the favorite, and take a little less on the underdog. This way the poor guy can feed his kids.

Incidentally, if you get your preliminary numbers out of the newspapers, chances are they'll be listed in a very strange way such as 6½-7. To make any sense out of *these* numbers simply insert a "5" between them and read it as 7 to 5 for the favorite and 6½ to 5 for the underdog. The second number, not the first, represents the favorite . . . apparently another scheme to confuse the bettor.

Baseball "Juice"

The sports book has tailored the structure of the odds payouts so that it earns a profit over long-term action. If the betting line is − 140 for the favorite, the underdog will go off at + 130, not + 140. In theory, the sports book breaks even when the favorite wins, and wins when the underdog wins. But sometimes it doesn't all work out as it should on paper. Yes, a sports book from time to time does indeed take a financial risk. Live by the sword . . .

All baseball lines are not all the same. I'm not talking about the actual numbers, but the juice that's in the numbers. Sure, the numbers do vary and that's important in terms of shopping for the best numbers. But the differences in the numbers also vary, specifically the difference between a favorite and underdog team. That difference, if you recall, is the sports book's profit. And it's worth shopping for also.

Let's say our line on the Mets/Red Sox game is − 140 Mets, + 130 Sox. This line is called a "dime-line" in sports book parlance, meaning that the difference between what the favorite *takes* from the bettor and what the underdog *gives* to the bettor is 10 cents. Remember to assess the line as − $1.40 and + $1.30 for simplicity sake and the 10 cents will become more evident.

Some sports books might offer a 15-cent line or 20-cent line instead, and you can be assured it means more profit for the sports book and less for the players. In our example, to make the line 15 cents the favorite Mets might be listed at − 145 and the Sox at + 130, or perhaps the extra juice will come from the underdog as − 140 Mets and + 125 Sox.

In order for the sports book to hold its percentages constant, more or less, the 10-cent betting line will become 20 cents when the favorite goes over − 200 (becomes greater than a 2 to 1 favorite). In fact, the 10-cent line becomes a 15-cent line at − 200 in order to prevent the sports book's profit from falling below 1%. The reason for this variation is not to deceive the bettor, nor to confuse him, but simply to maintain a reasonable profit level for the sports book.

As you can appreciate, if the difference between the numbers remained the same, while the numbers themselves became larger, then the percentage of difference would become *smaller*. The adjustment in the line is merely to prevent this from happening.

But don't be so naive as to think that all sports books follow this same schedule. It always pays to shop for the best numbers, *and* the best percentages.

Proving the Juice

LINE	ACTION
METS − 140	BETTOR A LAYS THE ODDS AT $140
SOX + 130	BETTOR B TAKES THE ODDS AT $100

SPORTS BOOK IS HOLDING $240,
IF UNDERDOG WINS, SPORTS BOOK NETS $10.
IF FAVORITE WINS, SPORTS BOOK BREAKS EVEN.

$$\frac{10}{240} = .04 \qquad \frac{.04}{2} = .02 = 2\% \text{ JUICE}$$

In determining the sports book's actual juice in baseball, we follow the same procedure as in football, except we must divide our number in half since the juice is only earned when the underdog wins. Over the long-term, the underdog wins about half the time. In football, the juice is earned regardless which side wins.

Baseball's juice computation reminds me of baccarat, where the "juice" is only applied to the banker-hand, *and only when it wins.* The hand is one of two nearly equal possibilities. Assuming the hand is bet about half the time, and indeed wins about half the time, we divide the juice of 5% by 4 (½ of ½), not 2, in order to approximate its actual cost to the player.

Baccarat belongs in the same breath with 10-cent baseball because it's the player's best game overall in the casino percentage-wise. Similarly, a 10-cent baseball line is the bettor's best game in the sports book, percentage-wise.

The Money-Line Vs.
The Point-Spread

Now we know that the sports book makes about 2½%
or less (2% average) on a 10-cent baseball line. If the line
is 20 cents, the sports book will make about 4½%, or
approximately the same as football and basketball. Yes,
in terms of percentages, baseball's 10-cent line is more
attractive than football or basketball, but doesn't get
anywhere near the overall action, in spite of the percentages, and the length of the season, and the number of
games.

Why not give baseball a point-spread you ask, as if to
suggest that the sports books must all be run by a bunch
of morons. Well, it's been tried, but not successfully.
And here's why.

First, baseball is a relatively low-scoring affair. It's difficult to pick a number that would equally divide the betting public. Secondly, there is more parity in baseball that
would make point-spreads unattractive. Thirdly, baseball has been based on odds, not points, since the days
of Abner Doubleday. Sports books that have tried a
baseball point-spread are plainly going against the grain.

And it works the other way too. Football and basketball would not be successfully wagered with a money-
line. Unlike baseball where most all teams have a reasonable chance of winning a particular contest, basketball
and football games are full of blow-outs—teams with vir-

tually no chance of winning. Such mismatches are most evident in college football where scores of 56-0 are not uncommon. With a money-line, who would want to take the underdog regardless of the odds payout. Even at +1000, or some such unheard of number, a team that could easily lose by 50+ points is not going to get my attention, or interest, or money! Even if the skies parted above South Bend, and Slippery Rock's players rode in on golden chariots . . . I'll still take Notre Dame!

But what if Slippery Rock got some points. Lots of points. Not odds. Points! Indeed, the point-spread can "even-up" virtually any two teams on the betting board. But sometimes the mismatches are so severe that the sports book doesn't want to offer it at *any* number. In such cases, the game goes off the board and only the teams slug it out. Today, it would be unusual to find a football or basketball point-spread on the board at 40 points or more, unless it's "circled."

A circled point-spread number means the sports book will take only limited action on that particular game. If there's any doubt about critical factors, such as a quarterback injury or bad weather, the betting limit might be greatly reduced. Similarly, if the game is a meaningless contest or if the teams are greatly mismatched, up goes the circle and down goes the bets. The sports book is simply protecting itself.

In some severe cases, the game might go off the board as indicated by an "X" in place of the point-spread, meaning that the game cannot be bet, at any amount. And here's another good reason for shopping. An "X" on the board in one sports book doesn't necessarily mean the game's off all over town, but that's probably what you'll find.

Your Ticket

Unlike an illegal bookmaker who usually takes a bettor's credit, Nevada sports books require *cash* at the window. In some cases, credit can indeed be established at Nevada sports books, but the stiff requirements, including minimum deposits and residency, usually preclude the small or out-of-town bettor from participating. In addition, there is some concern presently as to the merits and safeguards of the phone-account credit system.

In any event, assuming the bettor is playing with cash, a receipt for his wager is a "ticket" that might be handwritten or computer-printed. The ticket is more than a receipt however. If the ticket wins, or part of the ticket wins, it's almost as good as cash. Give your tickets the same respect.

Once your ticket is printed, you'll have locked in the odds or point-spread, even if the numbers change after you leave the window. The exception is in baseball when an "action" ticket is played and the listed pitchers do not start.

If you're an out-of-town player, most all sports books will accept mail delivery of your ticket and will remit the winnings by return mail. But check it out first. For example, Harrah's in Reno clearly states on their tickets: "WAGERS HONORED FOR ONE YEAR. WAGERS WILL NOT BE PAID BY MAIL." Of course, not only are the rules different among casinos, they also change. The smart bettor must learn how to read "the fine print," and ask questions when in doubt.

Don't be surprised or upset if the ticket writer asks for your name and address if you submit a large amount of cash. The new Nevada regulation, 6A, requires that sports books report large cash transactions to the Treasury Department. Most often, the sports book will try to keep track of large bets, even those under the $10,000 minimum amount for reporting, in case the bettor has more than one ticket played within 24 hours.

The idea behind regulation 6A is to discourage the "laundering" of illegal money in Nevada; changing little bills into big bills and so on. Everyone has to play by this rule, although no one likes it, especially the sports books themselves because of all the extra paperwork involved.

Other Bets

All three sports that we are concerned with: football, baseball, and basketball, offer the bettor a host of betting propositions other than simply picking against the money-line in baseball, or against the point-spread in football and basketball. Many pro-bettors concentrate exclusively on simply picking the winning teams. For the most part, they leave the other bets to the suckers. We're not going to dwell on these other bets because they really should not be recommended. But since they are a part of sports betting, this chapter would be incomplete without at least a cursory discussion.

TOTALS: Betting "the totals" is simply betting on the combined final score of both teams as being "over" or "under" a particular number. If you believe the game will be a low scoring contest, you would logically bet "under." If, on the other hand, you think the offenses will generate a lot of points, you would bet "over" the totals number. If the total score lands exactly on the totals number, all bets, either over or under, are returned to the player.

You should be made aware that the conditions on which a final score rests are very difficult to measure. Accordingly, some experienced bettors consider the totals as a frivolous wager and ignore that part of the betting line. The only possible exception is in professional basketball where the scoring potential of such few key players is more easily judged.

PARLAYS: If you want to show everyone in the sports book parlor that you're a rank amateur, walk up to the betting window and ask about making a parlay bet. But be careful. The guy might try to sell you a bridge, or a deed to a lost gold mine.

A parlay is nothing more than combining two or more games (usually up to 10) on one bet, in the hopes you'll win them all and . . . well, own your own gold mine. The payoff for picking 10 out of 10 winners is enticing. But like the million dollar slot jackpots and the $50,000 prize in keno, you're bucking big odds against you. A "realistic" parlay bet of two games should pay at 3 to 1 odds. Picking two winners out of two is indeed 3 to 1 odds.

$$(2 \times 2) - 1 \text{ to } 1$$

Your payoff on a two-game parlay however is 13 to 5, not the true 15 to 5 odds that you should be paid. The difference is juice, and plenty of it. How much? If the correct odds are 15 to 5 (3 to 1), yet we are only paid *13* to 5, we are shorted 2 units out of 20 (15 + 5).

$$\frac{2}{20} = .10 = 10\% \text{ juice!}$$

The odds against you climb even higher when you pick more games. Forget it!

Many sports books associated with casino-hotels distribute "parlay cards" throughout the casino, much like keno tickets. The cards list a selection of upcoming games (usually football), and all the player must do is mark his picks—against the spread of course—then sit back and watch his money disappear through the casino's "black hole." In most cases, ties lose. And if one game loses, the whole card is a loser. Such a deal!

The parlay card gimmick has been tried, or is being considered, by several states outside of Nevada as part of a legalized sports betting program, similar to state lotteries. Delaware gave it a shot in 1976, but it lasted only a few weeks because of a lot of snags, not the least of which was an NFL lawsuit against Delaware for "contaminating the game of football." But that's another story. I'm biting my tongue to spare you my own personal convictions about such narrow-minded thinking on the part of team owners and league executives.

To sum up, avoid parlays not because you're "contaminating" a sport, but because you're contaminating your wallet!

TEASERS: Here's another bet that's similar to a

parlay, but the sports book will let you add points to the point-spread (or subtract points) to make your picks stronger. What you are allowed to do is called "moving the line." The number of points you can move is usually 6 points in football and 4 points in basketball. If Dallas is favored over St. Louis by 10 points, you can take Dallas at −4 instead, or take St. Louis at +16! Sounds good, right?

Wrong! As you might expect by now, the payoffs are worse than the parlays. Instead of the true odds of 15 to 5, you might get 9 to 5. Juice? I'm not even going to figure it out. Yes, ties lose . . . and you'll lose your shirt, pants, socks and anything else of value if you're "teased" by these stupid bets.

ROUND ROBIN: Are you ready for this one? You can select up to four games, and parlay any two or any three, or go for all four winners. This reminds me of marking a "combination way ticket" in the keno parlor. And that's where it belongs. If you win two out of three, you might get a 3 to 5 payoff. On $5 you get $3! Is this legal?

HALF-TIME BETS: You guessed it. At half-time, the sports book will put up some new numbers for the second half, as if the second half was an entirely new game. It's a great way for the bettor to get his money back if the game isn't going exactly as he had planned. And it's a great way to lose twice the money you originally risked. The sports books are playing on the gambler's greed, a way to get back earlier losses. These guys are always looking for ways to take your money.

The danger of half-time betting should be obvious to anyone who's watched at least one football game in his entire lifetime. Have you ever watched a team get blown out in the first half, then come back and win it in the stretch? It's all a function of the coaches' famous half-time speeches. With half-time bets, we are not only concerned with rating the teams and the players, but now we have to rate the coaches. Incidentally, never make half-time bets against Notre Dame. The coach has his own speech-writer.

HOME-RUNS: To make this bet work for you, consult an astrological chart or get out your old ouija-board. It's really that silly. Surprisingly, a few sports books in Northern Nevada, and very few in Las Vegas are offering the home-run bet, based on a money-line such as −190 Kansas City and +170 Baltimore. Yes, it's a 20-cent line and "KC" is expected to hit more out of the park than the Orioles. So far, no sports book that I know of has a line out on grand-slams. The only saving grace for the sports bettor is that this line is only offered on baseball.

FUTURE BETS: At the beginning of a season, any season, the sports books will have all the teams listed on their board with the corresponding odds of winning the pennant, the World Series, The Super Bowl, The NBA Championship, The NCAA, you name it. Technically, the baseball All-Star game is considered a "futures" bet because the line goes up early. In some cases, the bettor can really clean up on long shots, such as the 1985/86 Chicago Bears at 15 to 1 odds. And when the NCAA basketball odds go up just when the 64 teams are announced, look out for the "cinderellas." If you follow college hoops, you know that invariably some unforeseen team makes it to the "Final 4." Nothing scares a book more than future bets, which is why the odds against the player are so high.

Incidentally, future bets usually generate the greatest line movement, and provide the bettor with a good reason to shop. But consider these bets only for fun, never for serious money.

Make Your Own Decisions

Time and time again, your gut instinct will tell you whether or not a spread is too high or too low; if a team is plowed under with problems, or fired up for a big game. You can determine in your own mind if that new quarterback is ready to face a national TV audience; is Seattle really as strong as they looked last week; is the so-called "bitter Rivalry" between Washington and Dallas really what it's cracked up to be; can the Rams play well in the snow; does Kansas City still have a chance for the playoffs?

Indeed, make these decisions yourself. But carefully. Put yourself in the position of the team, and the players. Make your decision without any TV analyst's help, without the sports handicapper's recommendation, and without your friend's bias. But make the decision *only if it's an easy one—an obvious choice.* If not, pass on it and try another game. There's no reason for picking a game other than the fact that for you, it was an easy, obvious decision. *Don't pick a game because it happens to be on TV, and you expect to be home watching it.* That's the worst reason of them all to bet a game. Some players bet a game because their favorite team is playing. That's another bad reason. Still, a few players bet any game without having *any* reason. Just to be "in action" I suppose. For this type of player, I suggest a consultation with his mother-in-law. Someone has to set him straight.

To make the decisions, it helps of course if you're knowledgeable of the sport. Your local newspaper's sports section is a good source of information, and so are the many fine sports magazines that are available. But remember, in doing so you're looking only for current data, not someone's biased selection.

Equally important, I recommend that you follow a particular team or conference, and consider only those teams for possible betting. If you live in the Midwest and follow the Big Ten, concentrate on only that conference. Forget UCLA or Arkansas if you know little about their team or conference. Sports bettors who are successful follow this important rule of exclusivity. *They give all their effort to a particular team or group of teams, and forget all the others.* Otherwise, there are simply too many teams, too many conferences, and too many players to keep abreast of.

Systems and Statistics

Ignore any systems or strategies that might have worked in the past, unless you can find someone stupid enough to take your bets on old games, convincing him that you honestly can't remember the scores. Remember, the only time a system works is after the games are over. *Believe me when I tell you that no one will ever be able to devise a system that will work for future games.*

These systems are based on statistics, and that's another area that needs to be discussed. Both systems and statistics are based on prior years and prior events, neither of which have much bearing on today's activity. For example, the Raiders' surprising record on Monday night games is merely a statistical anomaly. Nothing more. Using it as a basis for your decision is a mistake, for so many reasons, not the least of which is the sheer fact that most of the players who were around when the streak began have long since retired.

In so many cases of statistical analysis, years and years of results are fed into a computer and out comes the winner of tonight's game. How foolish! Not only do the players change (especially in college sports), but also the coaches, the managers, and even the cheerleaders. . . if that makes any difference. Even if many players did in fact remain on a particular team over a number of years, chances are their performance has changed, for better or worse, and at the very least they have aged. Nothing stays the same.

As you can see, with all the variables to consider, old statistics might be fun to compile, *but they lend very little to a game's predictability.*

The exception to all of this is of course *current* statistics. That's what I meant by reading newspaper or magazine accounts of particular teams you are following. But even these statistics are chancy at best. A team might start out weak, and finish the year winning their conference. Or a particular team rated high at the beginning of the season, may prove to be a big disappointment.

So-Called "Expert's" Advice

Sports services advertise in national newspapers and magazines, and even now you'll find them touting their selections on cable TV! Although a few might be reputable, many are fly-by-night organizations that pander to the gullible, desperate bettor who thinks of the service as a professional advisor, like an attorney or CPA. Not hardly. Anyone who has monitored these services over the years will know that their records, on average, are at best marginal, and arguably not worth their fee. Of course, there's always the possibility that some sports service will come along and turn up amazing results. But why take the chance? Besides, *a successful year doesn't mean a successful future.* It's the same as statistics and systems. A prognosticator's success last year certainly doesn't guarantee success *this* year. Each new season wipes the slate clean for everyone . . . the team, the player, *and* the analyst.

If you like to keep records, try keeping pre-season predictions from all the national magazines and sports experts who'll tell you who's going to win the college football championship, the pennant, the Super Bowl, and so on. This data is widely publicized and generally carries a lot of clout with bettors. All you have to do is keep the records for one season. And you'll never keep them again!

If it's too late to jot down pre-season selections, you can accomplish the same thing by taping any network pre-game show on your VCR. Watch the games and write down the scores. Then play back the tape and listen to the "expert" tell you why the Giants are sure to win. Of course, you'll have already known that the Giants lost 35-zip which makes the "expert" look like the village idiot.

This subject reminds me of the TV station down in Texas that recently promoted its football picks by having a chimpanzee actually select the teams. Unless you already know the story, I won't tell you how the chimp did, for fear you'll run out to your neighborhood pet store and order one.

To sum up, stay away from all sources of predictions. Even the "free" ones can be dangerous. In the case of those who charge a fee, understand that they're in it for the money. *Your* money!

The Line on Discipline

Remember to only bet the games that you believe have a decided advantage to you. **Never bet just for the sake of "being in action."** Be disciplined! If you can't get interested in a game unless you have "something riding on it," you have a problem that I can't help. And I'm willing to bet that you lose far more times than you win. If the game's on TV, watch it and enjoy it, *but don't bet it.* If I'm not getting through, promise me that you'll at least reduce your bet to the absolute minimum limit, but it's still a cop-out. **You must discipline yourself to go with only your strongest picks.** If you've looked at the lines and the entire weekend looks bleak, don't even open your wallet.

A tough example of this rule is the Monday night game during football season, the only game of the day. If it's a tough pick, pass! "Yes," you say, "but I'm going to be watching it!" So watch it! But don't bet it.

Still a better example of this pitfall is the Super Bowl, the last game of the season. Everyone has to bet it, right? Wrong! Not if it's a bad bet for you. If the pointspread is about where you would place it, and you can't move off center, enjoy the Super Bowl but (all in unison) DON'T BET IT!

The Super Bowl is a tough test of a bettor's discipline for other reasons too. Since it's the last game of the season, it might be a good chance to recoup your season losses, right? Maybe. Maybe not. If you're on the wrong side of the ledger, stay small, *don't try to recoup previous losses with one reckless bet.* Accept the fact that you've had a losing season and be done with it. The smart bettor, whether in the casino, at the race track, or in a sports stadium, follows this cardinal rule of betting: **Lay back when you're losing, but let your winnings run.** Never increase your bets when you're in the red; in fact, that's the time to reduce your wagers or quit. Let any winnings build safely, and increase the bets as you continue to win. It should be obvious, but *only a few gamblers have the discipline to structure their bets in relation to their winnings or losses.* Not only does the strength of the game determine the size of your bet, so does your season "standing" at that time. Are you "up," or are you "down"? Win or lose, it's a critical factor in determining your bet size.

Vulnerability

Not only must you be careful of your selections and careful of your bet size, but you must also be careful of your vulnerability. Let's say for example that you are going to bet four games next Sunday . . . four football games that you particularly like. For sake of example, let's say that each game is played at $100. Although you can't possibly believe that you might lose all four games, your vulnerability for that day *is* $400. If losing one or two hundred won't hurt you, but losing four hundred might sting a little, you're not using common sense. In fact, sting or no sting, it's not a good move and here's why. Regardless of how good your picks are, you might lose all four games. In fact, it's a statistical certainty that you will indeed lose four out of four games eventually, if you continually play four at a time. Without regard to any skill in your selection, the odds are 15 to 1 that you will lose all four (and your temper).

But more than that, betting all four games at once precludes you from structuring your bet size as your results become known. If the four games were bet over four different sessions, you could increase your bets if you win the first game, then the second, etc., or reduce your bets if you lost the first, the second, etc. By dumping all your action on one shot, you've prevented yourself from making any adjustment to your bet size.

Fractioning your total bet among four, five, or even six games is no assurance against anything. You're on the hook, and there *are* upsets. Be careful!

It's important to note that most pro bettors go with

one or two games per football weekend, maybe three at the most, and only then if the picks are all very, very strong. Are you that disciplined, or are you just a touch greedy? Are you mesmerized by the pleasant thought of winning all eight out of the eight games you just picked? Did you think about losing all eight?

Greed is the bookie's ally. Greed turns winners into losers. Be satisfied with a small, modest win, and start preparing for the next batch of games next week. No? You say that Sunday's early games are now over and you won two out of three. Now the late games are up and since you're ahead a little you might as well pick another one—a game that didn't particularly hit you at the start of the day. Three out of four sounds a lot better than two out of three, huh? Are you getting greedy? Are you betting recklessly? I wish I could take all of your action.

Actually, I don't. What I do wish however, is that you find the discipline to bet smartly and manage your money properly. Above all, **never make a bet that you can't comfortably afford to lose**. I said, *"Comfortably."* That doesn't mean having to hock the family car. You've heard it before and now you're hearing it again. It's the most important rule to follow. STAY WITHIN YOUR MEANS.

Study The Players

In basketball, a good study of the starting players is far more beneficial to the sports bettor than in any other sport. Why? *One player is 20% of the team on the floor!* If a bettor's research shows that a key player tends to play poorly in certain arenas (and this does happen) then the bettor has found a possible advantage over the bookmaker. Of course, if the oddsmaker knew the same thing the bettor knows, that factor will be built into the line, assuming the oddsmaker believes a large portion of the betting public is aware of it also.

In basketball, a sharp bettor who knows his business will spend considerable time on each individual player, more so than on the aggregate team, to try to find out things that the oddsmaker overlooked. The bettor will look beyond publicized injuries, reported disputes with the coach or other players, that sort of thing. What he's really looking for are personal things, such as a pending divorce that's not in the papers, a minor sickness, unreported financial problems, drugs, or even problems with the player's kids. Information of this type might seem difficult to acquire, but not really. The pro bettor has many contacts critical to his success and called upon often.

In baseball, there's no question that the pitchers get the most attention from the fans . . . and from the successful sports bettors too. Any decent bettor must study the pitchers carefully, for they have more influence on the line, and on your wagers, than any other factor.

If we are going to bet baseball like the pros do, we must always ask for "listed pitchers," when making our wager. This term means that our bet is on *only* if the two starting pitchers listed actually start the contest. If not, then we don't want the bet! Inexperienced bettors who show no concern about the pitchers (and obviously no concern about their money) make their bets in "action," meaning that the bet goes regardless of who's pitching.

Not smart.

Generally, the successful bettor is only interested in the pitcher's last three or four outings. Notice I said "the last three," not the last ten. The bettor should not even care about the early part of a season if he's nearing the play-offs. Pitchers change over the course of a season, as do all players. *What the bettor is looking for is a trend to consider, a trend that is timely and relevant to the upcoming game.* For those who don't keep such detailed records, many large newspapers routinely publish the listed pitchers and their records over the last three games. In most cases, the betting lines are also shown.

Similarly, football bettors will keep the same type of records about a quarterback's performance over the past three or four games. Trends of prior years are clearly of no interest, but trends over the past three games are obviously critical in predicting the quarterback's upcoming performance. No guarantees, mind you, but a telling trend that might, just might, continue.

The same factors that we cited earlier are also appropriate for the pitcher or quarterback as an individual, key player. His performance in certain stadiums, his mental attitude, personal problems, dissentions, etc., must never be discounted.

Line Bias

Another area of concern to the pro bettor deals with "regional" and "emotional" factors that might be plugged into a betting line. For example, oddsmakers know that San Francisco teams might be overly favored in Reno betting parlors, and similarly, Los Angeles teams in Las Vegas. If the bettor believes a line is unduly favored by a regional bias, he might be able to take advantage of the discrepancy. And then there are teams that always seem to get favorable attention . . . the sports bettor's "pets" so to speak. Teams such as Notre Dame, Dallas Cowboys, Chicago Bears, and even the Atlanta Hawks because of their cable network affiliation, tend to receive more than their share of favoritism. Such emotional factors can also become an advantage to the shrewd sports bettor who can detect the bias in the oddsmaker's lines.

And speaking of lines, many bettors are careful to watch for a movement in a line. If a line is moving away from his pending selection, he might talk with a sports book manager, or with other experienced bettors to find out why. Just as the sports book manager confers with other managers to strengthen and "tune in" a betting line, so do the bettors themselves who treat it seriously.

The experienced bettor knows that the bulk of factors that might lend predictability to the game have most likely been already applied to the opening line. Factors such as home-team underdogs (a favorite of unsuspecting bettors), West Coast to East Coast travel, let-downs, big games, interstate rivalries, etc., are almost always accounted for in the making of a line. Just knowing that puts the avid bettor at an advantage, by not applying the factor twice, or simply by knowing that the factor shouldn't have been counted in the first place.

Blow-Outs

A great many bettors concentrate on the non-conference college basketball and football schedule (the early season games) knowing that the oddsmakers are usually prevented from putting up "team-accurate" lines for likely blowouts. Either the games go off the betting board or the numbers simply are not enough. Maybe the lines are correct for dividing the bettors as they are supposed to do, but not high enough to accurately reflect the playing potential of two mismatched teams. If you're not afraid to give 30 points (the pro bettor isn't) you might find another "plum" in the oddsmaker's lines. If you're in doubt about this phenomena, read the college scores in the sports section Sunday morning, look for the mismatches, then look at the spreads and form your own conclusion. *For many bettors, these mismatches are money in the bank.*

Another trait of the seasoned bettor is in identifying the weakest lines among the different sports to be offered. In Barney Vinson's excellent book about the gambling scene, *Las Vegas Behind The Tables*, the author states, "It's been said that the really pro bettors concentrate on basketball, both pro and college, and on college football. It's also said that what the sports books lose on Saturday college football, they more than make up for on Sunday pro action. Apparently, the pros are less predictable."

It couldn't be said any better. **Most bookmakers agree that the weakest lines, in order, are: (1) early season college basketball, (2) college football, (3) pro basketball,**

(4) baseball, (5) pro football. And *you* probably spend most of your money, literally, knocking heads with the pros on Sunday!

The theory behind the listing also relates to what we covered earlier—the likelihood of mismatches and blow-outs. The parity among the pros is virtually a year-in, year-out affair. With the usual exceptions of course. The old axiom, "On any given Sunday . . ." does prove our point. Most any team is capable of beating any other. But try that out on UCLA vs. Utah State! The point is, Tampa Bay might not be the best team in the NFL but the team is made up of *pros*! Stand-outs in college. How the hell can you pick them?

Bet Size

Most pro bettors will compute the size of their next wagers after a careful plot of their win expectancy, based on their original stake and win/lose balances to date. To most of them, their methods are a proprietary matter. Nonetheless, we can assume that most of them follow the "Kelly Criterion" or an off-shoot of the formula that suggests the correct betting amounts based on a desired win percentage, original investment, number of bets, and anticipated earnings.

If you're starting with a $5,000 bankroll, it makes no sense to wager $2,500 on the first weekend of football. A wipe-out that weekend wipes out half of your stake! That's called the "Stupid Criterion," and works rather well if you're into charity.

As a general rule, the smart bettor will wager no more

than 3 or 4% of his original stake, based on a realistic winning percentage of maybe 57%. Any more than that is pure "pie in the sky."* Yes, just recognizing that fact is also the mark of a tough bettor . . . recognizing that he's not infallible. If you won three out of three this past weekend it doesn't mean you're invincible, it just means you did your homework. Hopefully, it didn't mean you were lucky. Luck doesn't make it in any form of gambling.

Another mark of a successful sports bettor is knowing when he's hot! And cashing it in for all it's worth. Like anything else, winners and losers in the sports bettor's record books come in streaks sometimes, and most often the streaks are tied to the bettor's proficiency at that particular time. A good streak-bettor, who's far ahead in the season already, might veer from his regimentized betting criteria and begin increasing his wagers 30 to 60%. He knows he's on the right track, betting back his winnings in pursuit of greater profits. Making large wagers when you're well ahead is the *only* time to do this. "Strike when the iron's hot," "Make hay while the sun shines," "When you're hot you're hot!" All these neat little phrases that mean the same thing do indeed apply

---

*In football or basketball, the bettor will break even against the point-spread by winning 52.3% of his games, assuming all bets are at the same level. That important percentage is easy to prove. Since the bettor must lay 11 to 10 odds, winning 11 games over the course of 21 yields our break even point: $11/21 = .523 = 52.3\%$. In a more empirical fashion, winning 11 games at $100 nets $1,100, and losing 10 games at $100 costs us $1,100 ($1,000 plus $100 juice).

There are only a few documented cases of a bettor winning more than 60% over the course of a season. As you can now see, any winning percentage over 52.3% can be considered successful.

here. The trick is having the determination, and the guts, to see it through. It might be easy betting $100 on a football game. But $200? $300? If you're up considerably (and I mean *considerably*), and a loss won't hurt you beyond your original expectations, yes, now's the time to increase the size of your wagers.

But streaks won't last forever. When it ends, count your winnings, go back to your original betting plans, and wait for another ride up.

Incidentally, this point reminds me of a common phrase that's heard around sports betting circles, "I'm in good shape, I'm betting with the bookie's money." NO! Your winnings are *your* money. Not the bookie's. That attitude can only lead to reckless, senseless losses. Your winnings are *your* money. It bears repeating.